Lake District Mountain Biking

ESSENTIAL TRAILS

Vertebrate Publishing, Sheffield
www.v-publishing.co.uk

Lake District Mountain Biking

ESSENTIAL TRAILS

Richard Staton & **Chris Gore**

Lake District Mountain Biking

ESSENTIAL TRAILS

 First edition published by Vertebrate Publishing in 2006, reprinted 2008.
Second edition published 2010, reprinted 2014. Third edition published 2021.

Vertebrate Publishing, Omega Court, 352 Cemetery Road,
Sheffield S11 8FT, United Kingdom.
www.v-publishing.co.uk

A CIP catalogue record for this book is available from the British Library.

ISBN 978-1-83981-073-2

Front cover: **Ewen Turner (front) and Pete Archer on the descent from Nan Bield Pass heading
towards Kentmere** (*route 22*) **© James Vincent.**
Back cover: **Ullswater singletrack** (*route 7*).
Photography by John Coefield, unless otherwise credited.

 All maps reproduced by permission of Ordnance Survey on
behalf of The Controller of Her Majesty's Stationery Office.
© Crown Copyright. 100025218.

Design by Jane Beagley, production by Cameron Bonser.
www.v-publishing.co.uk

Printed and bound in Europe by Pulsio.

Vertebrate Publishing is committed to printing on paper from sustainable sources.

MIX
Paper from
responsible sources
FSC® C128169

Contents

SECTION 1 – Classics

SECTION 2 – Epics

SECTION 3 – Enduros

SECTION 4 – Killers

SECTION 5 – Bonus Section

APPENDIX

ROUTE GRADES
▲ Easy ▲ Medium ▲ Hard (see page xi)

DOWNLOAD THE LAKE DISTRICT MOUNTAIN BIKING
GPX FILES FROM **www.v-publishing.co.uk/LDMB-GPX**

GATESCARTH PASS

Classics

Epics

Enduros

Killers

Bonus section

Lake District Mountain Biking

AREA MAP & ROUTE FINDER

CONTAINS ORDNANCE SURVEY DATA © CROWN COPYRIGHT AND DATABASE RIGHT

TOM FENTON DROPPING BACK INTO KENTMERE FROM THE GARBURN PASS

Introduction

Welcome to the third edition of this guidebook to mountain biking in the English Lake District. It's been a few years since we completed the first and second editions and, going off sales, thousands of mountain bikers are getting out there and enjoying the ride!

There's no doubt that mountain biking has changed. There is now a proliferation of 'trail centres' where you can park up, go for a ride on a fully waymarked trail which returns you back to your car and usually a cafe where you can sit and enjoy a pleasant latte. Nothing wrong with that, but hopefully this book will inspire riders to look beyond the obvious and go and do something different …

The routes are graded, but not just for technical difficulty and length. We have also considered how much navigation is required and how serious the mountain environment is through which the route passes. For example, we have given High Street a double black grade, not because the route is highly technical but because of the potential difficulties which could arise from poor navigation or rapidly changing weather conditions. For navigation, GPS devices have developed considerably and continue to do so; however, be aware of their limitations and get to know your unit! We recommend you still carry a good old-fashioned map and compass, especially useful if GPS batteries go flat!

On a less serious note we have maintained a good mix of rides, taking in the honeypots of Ambleside, to the magnificent forests of Whinlatter and Grizedale. But we were always keen to encourage exploration away from these areas, for example Miterdale and Whitbarrow Scar. Hopefully there is something for all tastes and abilities from short and technical to big mountain, singletrack to forest road – it's all in here!

We have revisited all the rides here and found them to be still as great now as when we first rode them. In terms of new additions we have added new routes at Nan Bield Pass and Grizedale. We've also recognised that riders are choosing ebikes and gravel bikes more and more so you'll find some guidance to suitable routes.

Richard Staton & Chris Gore

Acknowledgements

We would like to say thank you to a few people: Huw Davies, Paul Maine, Nick Cotton and Chris's wife Judith for suggesting routes and helping to ride them. Simon Young for his suggestions for some of the routes, and Keswick Bikes in general for helping out with broken bikes. Tom Fenton for editing the first edition and for writing up the routes in the North Lakes. Tim Russon, Tom Fenton, Jon Barton, Dave Balshaw and Charlie Smith for posing for photos, and John Coefield for his work in photographing them. Thanks also to Pete at Biketreks for the contacts. At Vertebrate Publishing, Jane Beagley and Cameron Bonser for their production work, and all of the team for their constant support.

How to use this book

RIDING IN THE LAKES

The Lake District is a high and mountainous region, and comes with all the dangers common to such regions. Do not rely on this guidebook alone, especially in adverse conditions – take a map and compass and know how to use them.

The trails in the Lakes rank as some of the hardest in the UK. Expect to shoulder your bike in places (possibly even on the descents!) – these are rocky and boggy mountain bridleways, not carefully planned man-made trails. Other than that, think about what we've said about safety on pages xiv–xv and enjoy some of the best riding in the UK!

THE ROUTES

This guide contains the best routes in the Lake District (in our opinion!). The aim is to encourage you to ride new trails in new areas, and to help you get to know the region. Try the routes as suggested, in reverse or joined to neighbouring rides. Once you've ridden a few and got to know what's what, you'll be able to link sections together to create your own rides.

Classics are generally fairly short (although not necessarily easy). **Epics** are a little longer and climb a little more. **Enduros** are a step up again, and the **Killers** are self-explanatory.

GRADES

Routes, climbs and descents are graded blue, red and black, in a similar system to that used at trail centres around the UK.

▲ Easy   ▲ Medium   ▲ Hard

Blue routes are generally shorter routes and are within reach of most MTBers, even newcomers, as well as the kind of thing you could do in a short day or when the weather's really foul. **Reds** are the kind of rides that won't actually take a full day, but you'll probably not want to do anything else once you've ridden them. And **Blacks** are those big and memorable days out that will demand endurance and some technical ability in places. These are the kind of routes to work up to.

The grades (and suggested route times) are based on average conditions – good weather and not too wet and muddy. In a drought the routes will feel easier; in the depths of winter, harder. Grades consider technicality, length, climbs, navigation, and remoteness – so one 'black' route might be a short all-out technical test while another could be a big endurance challenge with tricky navigation. As ever, these grades are subjective, as are our suggested times. How you find a particular route, downhill or climb will be dictated by your own levels of fitness and skill.

DIRECTIONS & ACCURACY

While every effort has been made to ensure accuracy within the directions in this guide, things change and we are unable to guarantee that every detail will be correct. Please treat stated distances as guidelines. **Please exercise caution if a direction appears at odds with the route on the ground. A comparison between direction and map should see you on the right track.**

Rights of Way

Countryside access in the UK hasn't been particularly kind to cyclists, although things are improving. We have 'right of way' on bridleways and byways. However, having 'right of way' doesn't actually mean having the right of way, just that we're allowed to ride there – so please give way to walkers and horse riders. We're also allowed to ride on green lanes and some unclassified roads, although the only way to determine which are legal and which aren't is to check with the local countryside authority. Obviously, cycle routes are also in.

The very understanding Forestry Commission generally allows cyclists to use its land (again, you'll need to check with them first to be sure). You must, however, obey all signs, especially those warning of forestry operations – a fully loaded logging truck will do more than scuff your frame …

Everything else is out of bounds (unless, of course, the landowner says otherwise). Riding illegally can upset walkers (who have every right to enjoy their day) and is, in many cases, technically classed as trespass (meaning you could be prosecuted for any damage caused). Not all tracks are signed, so it's not always obvious whether that great-looking trail you want to follow is an 'illegal' footpath or a 'legal' bridleway. That's why it's a good idea to carry a map with you on every ride.

The bike

Generally any half-decent mountain bike will be fine for riding in the Lakes. For the harder routes, a full-suspension bike could add comfort and control, while a lightweight race bike might make the hills easier.

Check everything's working – especially for harder riding. You won't be going uphill fast if your gears seize but may be quicker than planned if your brakes don't work. Pump the tyres up, check that nothing's about to fall off or wear through and check that everything that should be tight is tight. The Lakes are always rocky and often boggy, so go big and knobbly, tyre-wise.

GRAVEL BIKES

Gravel bikes are the new 'adventure' bike, offering versatility well beyond that of a traditional road racing or touring bike. Most will now take a tyre well beyond 40mm width and, with advances in geometry, flared bars and even dropper posts, they can hold their own off-road while still being fast on the black top. The Lake District does offer opportunities for gravel riding, especially in Grizedale Forest, Claife Heights and the easier bridleways around South Lakeland. We've highlighted some suitable routes in the guide to get you going.

EBIKES

The arrival of ebikes has opened up mountain biking to more people than ever before and for a variety of reasons, which is a good thing and good for the sport. Even seasoned mountain bikers have made the switch as it enables climbs, which were once a walk, to be ridden, greater distances to covered or simply more descent to be enjoyed.

As the technology advances, they will become lighter and offer even more versatility and range. We've highlighted some routes that we feel really lend themselves to ebikes, either because of distance or the climbs involved, sometimes both! However, please be aware that some Lakeland routes do involve carries on steep, rocky ground so, whatever bike you have, make sure you're able to do so before setting out.

Routes suitable for gravel bikes	Routes suitable for ebikes
3 Cartmel Fell	16 Helvellyn
10 Troutbeck & Jenkin Crag	21 Walna Scar
11 Ings & Winster	24 High Street

Essential kit

HELMET

The best helmet is the one that you're wearing. Make sure it fits, you're wearing it correctly and that it won't move in a crash.

CLOTHING

You need to get your clothing right if you want to stay comfortable on a bike, especially in bad weather. The easiest way to do this is to follow a layering system. Begin with clothing made from technical synthetic or wool fabrics that will wick the sweat away from your body and then dry quickly, keeping you dry and warm. Stay away from cotton – it absorbs moisture and holds on to it. If it's chilly, an insulating layer will keep you warm, and a wind/waterproof layer on the outside protects from the elements. Layers can then be removed or added to suit the conditions. Padded shorts are more comfortable, but the amount of Lycra on display is up to you. Baggy shorts, full length tights and trousers are all available to match the conditions. Set off a little on the cold side – you'll soon warm up. Don't leave the warm clothes behind though, as the weather can turn quickly.

GLOVES

Gloves ward off blisters and numb hands and help keep your fingers warm. They also provide a surprising amount of protection when you come off.

FOOTWEAR

Flat pedals/clipless – it's your call. Make sure you can walk in the shoes and that they have sufficient tread for you to do so. Consider overshoes if it's chilly.

OTHER ESSENTIALS

As mentioned, take any necessary spares, tools, tube and pump, spare clothes, first aid kit, food and water. Stop short of the kitchen sink, as you'll still want to be able to actually ride your bike. You'll need something to carry this lot in. We'd suggest a hydration pack, as they allow you to drink on the move and keep excess weight off the bike.

General safety

The ability to read a map, navigate in poor visibility and to understand weather warnings is essential. Don't head out in bad weather, unless you're confident and capable of doing so.

Some of the routes described point you at tough climbs and steep descents that can potentially be very dangerous. Too much exuberance on a steep descent in the middle of nowhere and you could be in more than a spot of bother, especially if you're alone. Consider your limitations and relative fragility.

Be self-sufficient. Carry food and water, spares, a tube and a pump. Consider a first aid kit. Even if it's warm, the weather could turn, so take a wind/waterproof. Think about what could happen on an enforced stop. Pack lights if you could finish in the dark.

If you're riding solo, think about the seriousness of an accident – you might be without help for a very long time. Tell someone where you're going, when you'll be back and tell them once you are back. Take a mobile phone if you have one, but don't expect a signal. And **don't** call out mountain rescue because you've grazed your knee.

Riding in a group is safer (ambitious overtaking manoeuvres excepted) and often more fun, but don't leave slower riders too far behind and give them a minute for a breather when they've caught up. Allow extra time for a group ride, as you'll inevitably stop and chat. You might need an extra top if you're standing around for a while. Ride within your ability, make sure you can slow down fast and give way to other users. Bells might be annoying, but they work. If you can't bring yourself to bolt one on, a polite 'excuse me' should be fine. **On hot, sunny days, slap on some Factor 30+ and** ALWAYS WEAR YOUR HELMET!

In the event of an accident

In the event of an accident requiring immediate assistance dial **999** and ask for **POLICE** or **AMBULANCE**. If you can supply the services with a six-figure grid reference of exactly where you are it should help to speed up their response time.

EMERGENCY RESCUE BY SMS TEXT

Another option in the UK is contacting the emergency services by SMS text – useful if you have a low battery or intermittent signal, but you do need to register your phone first. To register, simply text 'register' to 999 and then follow the instructions in the reply. Do it now – it could save yours or someone else's life. **www.emergencysms.net**

Rules of the (off) road

1. Always ride on legal trails.
2. Ride considerately – give way to horses and pedestrians.
3. Don't spook animals.
4. Ride in control – you don't know who's around the next corner.
5. Leave gates as you find them – if you're unsure, shut them.
6. Keep the noise down and don't swear loudly when you fall off in front of walkers.
7. Leave no trace – take home everything you took out.
8. Keep water sources clean – don't take toilet stops near streams.
9. Enjoy the countryside and respect its life and work.

STICKS PASS, HELVELLYN (ROUTE 16)

Planning your ride

1. Consider the ability/experience of each rider in your group. Check the weather forecast. How much time do you have available? Now choose your route.
2. Study the route description before setting off, and cross-reference it with the relevant map.
3. Bear in mind everything we've suggested about safety, clothing, spares and food and drink.
4. Get out there and get dirty.

Maps & symbols

Ordnance Survey maps are the most commonly used, are easy to read and many people are happy using them. If you're not familiar with OS maps and are unsure of what the symbols mean, you can download a free map legend from **www.ordnancesurvey.co.uk**

We've included details of the relevant OS map for each route. To find out more about OS maps or to order maps please visit **www.ordnancesurvey.co.uk**

Here's a guide to the symbols and abbreviations we use on the maps and in our directions:

DESCENDING LOWER MAN, HELVELLYN (ROUTE 16)

Section 1

Classics

A quick blast after work, a night loop you can finish before your lights die, or a ride to squeeze in when you're short of time. That's a classic. Relatively low on distance and never taking you too far from the start, these are still good, solid rides. Short but not necessarily easy.

STARTING THE CLIMB UP GARBURN PASS FROM KENTMERE (ROUTE 4)

LONSCALE FELL (ROUTE 6)

Introduction

A great ride for those looking for some decent mountain biking but wanting to avoid the rigours of anything too technical. It is also a good ride for avoiding the hotspots of the Lake District – it really does feel remote on Woodland Fell and Subberthwaite Common.

The Ride

This route takes an anticlockwise course from Blawith on quiet lanes, farm tracks and some great singletrack. The views on Woodland Fell are fantastic, as is the descent off the fell. At Spunham, the ride takes you along tracks and quiet lanes with a stiff climb before another bridleway takes you over Subberthwaite Common. After Birch Bank Farm the trails become a little vague, but continue east to Kiln Bank and Raisthwaite Lane before heading back to Blawith.

ALTITUDE PROFILE

GREEN MOOR BECK

BLAWITH LOOP   **GRADE:** ▲

TOTAL DISTANCE: 12KM/7 MILES » **TOTAL ASCENT**: 368M/1,207FT » **START/FINISH**: BLAWITH CHURCH
START GR: SD 288883 » **PARKING**: IN FRONT OF BLAWITH CHURCH » **TIME**: 1–2 HOURS » **SATNAV**: LA12 8EQ
OS MAP: LANDRANGER 96 » **PUB**: RED LION, LOWICK BRIDGE, TEL: 01229 885 366 » **CAFE**: BLUEBIRD CAFE, CONISTON, TEL: 01539 441 649.

Directions – Blawith Loop

➲ From the church in Blawith, take the lane opposite, heading west, bearing **R** at the fork. At the next fork after a cattle grid bear **R** again (the left fork is signed *Tottlebank Only*). After 800m the road reaches a T-junction.

2 Turn **R** then immediately **L** on to a bridleway signed *Woodland & Cumbria Way*. Follow the bridleway – superb riding – **ignoring** turnings until you reach the highest point of Woodland Fell amidst stunning scenery. At the bridleway fork soon afterwards, bear **R** and head downhill. A great descent takes you to Green Moor. **Don't cross** the river, but keep **L** heading south and uphill. The track levels off and then descends to join a farm track at Spunham.

3 Turn **L** along this track, **ignoring** all turnings, to join a metalled road. Turn **R** and then **L** at the junction, signed *Grizebeck*. Follow this road south for 1.7km to a junction. Turn sharp **L** (**ignore** the bridleway signed *Tottlebank* on the left), climbing steeply up the hardest climb on the route. Turn **L** on to a bridleway at a sharp right-hand bend shortly before the road begins to descend. The bridleway runs east past a small tarn, becoming a little vague – don't worry, just keep heading east.

4 At the road, go **SA** down the lane opposite, almost immediately turning **L** on to a lane leading to Birch Bank Farm. Turn **L** on to a bridleway just in front of the farm and turn **R** through the first gate reached after a small rise (the track ahead goes on to Tottlebank). Quickly pass through two more gates and follow the vague bridleway, keeping the wall to your right and heading east. At Mill Moss, go through another gate and join a better trail. Follow this to the buildings at Kiln Bank, **dismount** and walk **SA** through the farmyard (signed *Cumbria Way*) on to the tarmac of Long Lane. Descend to a T-junction and turn **L** back to Blawith.

◄●○ **Making a day of it**
Head north-east from Blawith to reach the wonderful Grizedale Forest (options include the **Grizedale Loop** (page 85), **Grizedale & Esthwaite** (page 107) or **The North Face Trail** (page 164)).

01 Blawith Loop

CLIMBING UP FROM FAR SAWREY

02 Claife Heights

Introduction

A ride around Claife Heights really is an ideal introduction to Lakes riding: a ferry ride on Windermere, a trolley along the scenic shores of the lake and then steady riding on wide tracks with some good climbs and superb downs (not too scary) on open land. We have also given you a choice of finishes: either stop at the Cuckoo Brow Inn for a pint and a short ride back to the ferry on the road, or take the more technical return route over Claife Heights and on to a great downhill (a bit more technical). This route would make a great evening ride, or a nice family outing with picnic potential at Moss Eccles Tarn.

The Ride

Starting from the ferry, the ride follows the picturesque west shore of Windermere, passing Belle Isle and various moored yachts (depending on time of year) and up to Belle Grange. The route then heads inland to High Wray and takes forestry tracks past Basecamp outdoor centre. Steady climbing on generally good tracks leads to Claife Heights, with each uphill followed by a good descent. The run down from Claife Heights is one of these: a fantastic rolling downhill through open land that carries you past various tarns to eventually bring you out at the Cuckoo Brow Inn. From here, head back to the ferry, either directly along the road or, a better option, over to Harrow Slack, via an uphill start and a great technical descent.

ALTITUDE PROFILE

(Altitude profile chart showing route from 0 Km to 15 Km, Metres axis 40 to 230, with labels CLAIFE HEIGHTS and FAR SAWREY)

CLAIFE HEIGHTS   GRADE: ▲

TOTAL DISTANCE: 15KM/9 MILES » **TOTAL ASCENT**: 512M/1,680FT » **START/FINISH**: FERRY PORT ON WEST SIDE OF WINDERMERE » **START GR**: SD 391957 » **PARKING**: AT FERRY (EXPENSIVE) OR LIMITED PARKING ON THE WEST SHORE OF WINDERMERE » **TIME**: 1–2 HOURS » **SATNAV**: LA22 0LZ » **OS MAP**: LANDRANGER 97 » **PUB**: CUCKOO BROW INN, FAR SAWREY, TEL: 01539 443 425; OR NUMEROUS OTHERS IN BOWNESS-ON-WINDERMERE » **CAFE**: NUMEROUS IN BOWNESS-ON-WINDERMERE.

🏁 From the ferry go **SA** on a metalled road, turning **R** at the road junction on a left-hand bend by the lake, heading north along the west shore of Windermere. After the second cattle grid, the road turns to track. Follow this (great undulating riding) for 2km to Belle Grange. Go **SA**, **ignoring** the bridleway on the left, following bridleway signs to *High Wray*.

2 At the metalled road by the car park, follow the road uphill, **ignoring** the bridleway on the right. The road goes through the farm at Beyond Fields to a junction. Turn **L**, then, after 20m, turn **L** again on to a dirt track signed *Basecamp*, with a bridleway signed *Claife Heights*.

3 The track continues uphill. At the fork, bear **R** and go through a gate with many padlocks, following the bridleway signed *Guide Posts*. As you crest a rise and start to descend, bear **R** at the fork. Go **SA** at the crossroads on to a bridleway signed *Ferry/Far Sawrey*.

4 Turn **R** at the next crossroads on to a bridleway signed *The Sawreys*. This is not obvious – the track ahead looks good but is only a footpath, while the track you need looks narrow, steep and uninviting. For the strong, it is a harsh ride, while for others it is a short push. At the junction with a wider trail, turn **R** and follow the track to a gate. Go through the gate and enjoy the undulating but mainly downhill ride past the tarns and livestock.

5 At the fork, bear **L** through the gate signed *Far Sawrey*. Turn **R** at the metalled road and then **L** at the junction with the main road. (Stop off at the Cuckoo Brow Inn for a quick drink and a bite to eat, and then take the quick **OR** route back to the ferry by following the main road all the way to the lake.)

6 Turn **L** on to the bridleway by the phone box and follow the trail uphill. After the first gate, bear **R** at the fork, still heading uphill. At the next gate, go **SA**, still on the bridleway. After one more gate, start a fun and technical downhill, which leads back down to your outward route along the shore of Windermere. Turn **R** and retrace your steps to the ferry.

🔗 **Making a day of it**
A short distance on the road will take you to Grizedale Forest. Try the **Grizedale Loop** on page 85, the purpose-built singletrack or one of the family trails there.

p85, p107, p164
Grizedale Forest routes

02 Claife Heights

03 Cartmel Fell

18km/11 miles

Introduction

This is a hidden gem of a ride, taking in the tracks and trails around the Cartmel Fell area and the forest of Chapel House Plantation. This area is seldom visited by the hordes of bikers and walkers found in the main areas of the Lakes and is a pleasure to ride. The road riding does little to detract from this route as it is on quiet roads and lanes. This is not a technically hard ride, so would suit those aspiring to improve their bike skills, especially if the extra loop to Staveley-in-Cartmel is taken.

The Ride

From the car park, a steep bit of tarmac soon plateaus, then it's downhill with some sharp bends to Strawberry Bank. A quiet road heads off to Cartmel Fell but a bridleway is taken before this is reached. A generally good bridleway is followed over fells and through woods to the picturesque Sow How Tarn. A little further on and the ride joins Sow How Lane. A short blast downhill through Foxfield ensues before fantastic undulating terrain to Simpson Ground. From here the ride leads to Chapel House Plantation, with some good singletrack leading on to forestry roads. There is a choice of finishes: either follow the forestry roads back to Sow How Lane and Gummer's How, or downhill singletrack taking you to Staveley-in-Cartmel, then back up the forestry roads to join the other finish.

ALTITUDE PROFILE

250

STRAWBERRY BANK

SOW HOW

CHAPEL HOUSE PLANTATION

Metres

50

0 Km   3   6   9   12   15   18

CARTMEL FELL　　　　　　　　　　　　　　　　　　　　　**GRADE:** ▲

TOTAL DISTANCE: 18KM/11 MILES » **TOTAL ASCENT**: 700M/2,297FT » **START/FINISH**: GUMMER'S HOW CAR PARK
START GR: SD 389876 » **PARKING**: GUMMER'S HOW CAR PARK » **TIME**: 1.5–2.5 HOURS » **SATNAV**: LA12 8NW
OS MAP: LANDRANGER 97 » **PUB**: MASONS ARMS, CARTMEL FELL, TEL: 01539 568 486 » **CAFE**: FELL FOOT NATIONAL
TRUST CAFE, TEL: 01539 531 273.

S➜ Turn **R** out of the car park and grind uphill for a short distance. This tends to hurt the lungs and legs if you don't warm up, but it is soon over. **Ignore** all turnings until you reach a very fast downhill, topped off with some very tight bends near Strawberry Bank – be careful!

2 Go past the Masons Arms (or stop if you feel the need) and, just after a left-hand bend, turn **R** signed *High Newton, Cartmel Fell*. Follow this pleasant lane downhill. Pass a phone box and a footpath signed *Pool Garth* on the left and climb steeply round a right-hand bend. Just after this, turn **R** through a gate (there are two other gates on the opposite side of the lane).

3 After a short steep stretch, the track splits. Fork **L** through a gate on to a bridleway signed *Sow How*. After the gate the track appears to split again – follow the **R** fork.

4 Follow the grassy bridleway to an unmarked T-junction and turn **R**. Pass through a gated wall and continue **SA**, passing to the **R** of Heights Cottage. Follow the bridle-way back **L** (signed) following the wall, and go through a gate into the woods, then through another gate and out of the woods. The very picturesque Sow How Tarn is in front of you; unfortunately this is privately owned, so carry on and bear **L** in front of the Tarn (signed), which then brings you to a T-junction with Sow How Lane.

5 Turn **L** and go through a gate to reach Foxfield and a metalled lane. **Ignore** turnings and stick to the road. After a downhill in the woods go through a gate and, after 150m, turn **R** on to a track, crossing under the electricity lines.

6 After a short distance, go through two gates; the great undulating track leads to Simpson Ground. Turn **R** at the T-junction – bridleway signed *Staveley-in-Cartmel*, go through the gate and into the woods, this is Chapel House Plantation.

7 Turn **L** on to the first wide trail going uphill – if you arrive at the reservoir, you've missed it! A great piece of singletrack runs through the woods and ends at the forestry road.

03 **Cartmel Fell**

8 Turn **R** on the forest road. On a sharp left-hand bend, turn **R**, bearing **L** where the track forks a little further on (to the right is a marked footpath). An overgrown forestry track gives some good riding.

> **OR** Turn **L** along the forestry road and, after a short distance, turn **R** on a left-hand bend on to a signed bridleway. A steep, bouldery and technical trail ends at a forest road. Go **SA** over this and through a deer gate to follow singletrack through the scrub. After the next deer gate, the track crosses open fell and descends through the woods to Staveley-in-Cartmel. At the road by the phone box, turn **L** and follow the road to Chapel House Wood car park. Turn **L** uphill on to the forestry road, pass the bridleway crossroads that you previously came down and continue to a sharp right-hand bend. Go **SA** to rejoin the main route.
>
> **Note:** This is a forestry road and can be out of commission at any time due to work being carried out within the forest.

9 At the T-junction, turn **L** and follow the track to a double gate. Go through this and on to the road – this is Sow How Lane. Turn **L** and ride to a T-junction. Turn **L** again and back to the car park.

⊷◌◯◠ **Making a day of it**

There are some pleasant bridleways to the north of this ride, towards Bowness. Follow the road north from Strawberry Bank to find them.

DOUBLETRACK PAST SOW HOW TARN

04 Garburn Pass

15km/9 miles

Introduction

A great little route, crossing one of the classic Lakeland passes. Off-road for the vast majority of its length, the route features some seriously technical climbing (and descending, if you take the option of reversing it) and some fast, fun descents. A route for experienced riders, crossing high mountain country. The main feature of the route is most definitely the climb up the Garburn Road from Kentmere. You might clean it, you might stop and play around until you conquer individual sections, or you may very well end up shouldering your bike. Believe me, it's worth it in the end! Reversing the route gives an easier climb and a more technical descent.

The Ride

Starting from Ings, the route climbs the hill over to Kentmere. A brief section of tarmac, a couple of tricky sections of climbing, some wide lines and a little rolling singletrack lead to the fast descent to Kentmere Hall. The route then heads out of the valley up one of the Lake District's most famous old roads, Garburn Pass. It's rocky, it's steep and it's long. If you can clean this then you're doing well! The climb is soon rewarded with a fantastic decent down into Troutbeck. Try to stay onboard as you attempt to look at the magnificent view and look where you're going at the same time! Either reverse the route (recommended) or drop easily on tarmac to Ings.

GARBURN PASS   GRADE: ▲

TOTAL DISTANCE: 15KM/9 MILES » **TOTAL ASCENT:** 476M/1,562FT » **START/FINISH:** WATERMILL INN, INGS
START GR: SD 444987 » **PARKING:** ROADSIDE PARKING IN INGS (PARKING MAY BE LIMITED, PARTICULARLY AT WEEKENDS); PLEASE PARK RESPONSIBLY » **TIME:** 2 HOURS » **SATNAV:** LA8 9PY
OS MAP: LANDRANGER 90; LANDRANGER 97 » **PUB:** WATERMILL INN, INGS, TEL: 01539 821 309
CAFE: WILF'S CAFE, STAVELEY, TEL: 01539 822 329.

Directions – Garburn Pass

S→ From the Watermill Inn (at the Ambleside/western end of Ings), cross the A591 and head up Grassgarth Lane. Climb the lane for 600m to a bridleway on the **R**, with the caravan site visible down to your left. Follow the bridleway, climbing easily at first, but then with more difficulty near the top, to a gate.

2 Pass through the gate and follow the walled track to the **L**, continuing uphill. The bridleway soon reaches the top by Hugill Hall. Turn **L** on to a road just after the farm and follow the track sharply **L** past the buildings. Climb on a walled track in the direction of Kentmere, passing a metalled lane on the right from Browfoot.

3 At the T-junction, turn **R** and continue until you reach two gates. Take the gate on the **R** towards Kentmere Hall, following the bridleway alongside the wall. Eventually reach a gate in the wall and pass through it, continuing **SA** alongside the wall. Follow the bridle-way to a gate, where the trail finally leaves walls and gates behind for a little while and climbs out across the fell. Follow this bold path and cross a stream to another gate.

4 Go through the gate and follow the bold path, hugging the wall, to the start of the ripping descent to Kentmere Hall. **Please** be aware of potential hazards on this descent: walkers, sheep and other mountain bikers climbing up. There are also a couple of gates, sometimes open, sometimes not. High speed can be achieved, but make sure you can stop or slow down in time.

5 The gate at Kentmere Hall is soon reached. Go through the gate and turn **R**, taking the farm track away from the hall. A short climb leads to the church and the road. Turn **L**. Follow the road, bearing **L** at a fork (the right-hand option is closed with a gate). Continue for a short distance and turn **R** on to a wide, rocky track by a house – this is Garburn Road.

6 After a brief effort you reach a gate. Continue through the gate to start the climb proper. How far can you get before exhaustion or the difficulty of the 'road' beats you? The continuation of strict 4x4 bans has resulted in the pass suffering far less erosion problems and it is therefore a lot more ridable – but in no way less challenging! Hard men and women claim to be able to ride all the way to the top without dabbing. If this is your mindset then what are you waiting for? If you're **really** hard you could plant an axe in your head first!

04 **Garburn Pass**

7 After some effort – perhaps you walked bits, perhaps you didn't (it really doesn't matter) – you reach the top gate. Continue through and the 'road' bears **L**, to another gate and the start of the descent. As with the descent to Kentmere Hall, be aware of other users climbing uphill. There are some tricky sections that can catch out even the best of riders so please take care!

8 At the bottom gate you have a choice: turn around and do the pass again, reversing the route back to Ings (recommended), or continue **SA** and finish quickly on tarmac. Continuing, follow the track through the gate to a fork. Take the **L** (uphill) track, following it past Dubbs Reservoir on the right and down to the road.

9 Turn **L**, bearing **L** at the fork. Continue down the hill to a right-hand bend, a short climb and a drop down to the main road. Turn **L** and use the cycle path to return to Ings and a well-earned beverage.

◄◯◯ **Making a day of it**
For starters, ride the route as a there and back – the pass is worth it. Then link it to the **Kentmere & Longsleddale** route on page 43.

05 Black Combe

14km/9 miles

Introduction

A real esoteric gem. Out on the coast, this great little hill gives spectacular views, weather permitting, out over the Irish Sea towards the Isle of Man, and inland towards most of the Lakeland peaks. A testing climb on very good tracks up a 600-metre peak – no technical ability required, just big thighs! The downhill is, as always, the reward for your hard work – on open fells with great views out to sea. Route finding is very easy on a clear day, but as Black Combe is on the coast, clouds can quickly amass around the summit. When this happens, the vague paths that are usually so easy to see in the distance all but disappear into the mist, so either take a compass or wait for a clear day.

The Ride

This route starts at Townend Hall on the A595 to give the legs a short warm-up, before the onslaught of Black Combe begins in earnest. From Whicham the bridleway kicks uphill to Black Combe. The riding is technically easy, but runs straight up a very big hill. Good tracks lead to the rounded summit with a shelter and trig point, from where the spectacular views can be admired. The path takes a close call to Blackcombe Screes before heading off downhill to Hall Foss, with distracting views out across the sea. A great bit of riding under Black Combe and parallel to the A595 leads back to Whitbeck and then on to your transport.

ALTITUDE PROFILE

590

Metres

BLACK COMBE

40

0 Km   2   4   6   8   10   12   14

BLACK COMBE   GRADE: ▲

TOTAL DISTANCE: 14KM/9 MILES » **TOTAL ASCENT**: 681M/2,234FT » **START/FINISH**: TOWNEND HALL
START GR: SD 119839 » **PARKING**: LAY-BY AT TOWNEND HALL » **TIME**: 2 HOURS » **SATNAV**: LA19 5UR
OS MAP: LANDRANGER 96 » **PUB**: PRINCE OF WALES, FOXFIELD, TEL: 01229 716 238 » **CAFE**: BOOTLE.

Directions – Black Combe

S From the lay-by at Townend Hall turn **L** on to the A595 towards Whicham. At Whicham, follow the road to the **L**, signed *Broughton* (**ignore** the A5093 which continues straight ahead to Millom). After 700m, take the first **L** shortly after a lay-by up a small road, passing the old school and a church. After the last building the road turns to track. Bear **R** as the track splits shortly afterwards (straight ahead is a footpath). Ride to a gate and select your lowest gear ...

2 The bridleway ahead is very good but very steep. The hardest section is the start up to Townend Knotts. Thereafter it is less steep (compared with what you have just ridden), but your legs are more tired so keep pumping. At the summit there is a trig point and a stone shelter – this can be a windy place with a stiff breeze coming in off the Irish Sea.

3 Continue **SA** over the summit on a vague track – if visibility is good there should be no problem – passing close to Blackcombe Screes on the right, before striking off to the **L** (north/north-west) and becoming more defined. **Ignore** the path going off right (north-east) to Hentoe Hill, which is easily taken in poor conditions. It's vague and leads on to Whitecombe Screes – so if you are on near-vertical scree slopes for a continued period you are off route!

4 A sheep-scattering descent across open fell eventually leads to a wall. Turn **L**, following the wall and fence. Ford the stream at Hall Foss, and the somewhat deeper stream at Holegill Beck. An undulating bridleway leads through to Whitbeck Mill and back to Townend Hall.

Making a day of it
This is a fairly isolated route, although it could be linked to the **Walna Scar** area if you're up for a lot of road riding.

05 Black Combe

DAVE BALSHAW ON LONSCALE FELL

06 Two from Keswick
– Lonscale Fell Loop & Skiddaw

19km/12 miles
16km/10 miles

Introduction

Keswick is the only big(ish) town in the Northern Lakes. It's easy to reach, has bike shops, pubs, cafes and a pencil museum. As a result, lots of people head there, which can cause problems with parking (there are at least two other car parks along this route if you can't find a space in Keswick) and may mean annoyingly busy trails. Don't worry – these routes are still worth doing. They are both relatively short, so early morning or evening bashes are a real possibility. The Lonscale Fell Loop is a relatively easy offering for the Northern Lakes. It involves only a little technical riding and is great fun. The Skiddaw route is slightly different. Look north from Keswick. See that enormous hill? Now carry your bike up it and slide back down.

The Ride

The Lonscale Fell Loop leaves Keswick along the old railway line, crossing some massive north shore stuff (tongue firmly in cheek) on the way. Steep road work gets most of the climbing out of the way before a track runs up into the hills. Things get technical as you descend to ford Glenderaterra Beck, and you'll be doing well if you ride the return leg in one. Technical singletrack leads back down the valley to a fast descent (walkers permitting) into Keswick.

To tackle Skiddaw, grind up and out of Keswick. From there you'll probably manage to ride for about another kilometre before you're off and pushing. Carry/push/ride – whatever you can manage – to the top and then tackle the loose stone descent at whatever speed you feel happy with.

TWO FROM KESWICK: LONSCALE FELL & SKIDDAW   GRADE: ▲

TOTAL DISTANCE: 19KM/12 MILES (06A), 16KM/10 MILES (06B) » **TOTAL ASCENT**: 400M/1,312FT (06A), 925M/3,035FT (06B)
START/FINISH: KESWICK » **START GR**: NY 266236 » **PARKING**: OTLEY ROAD CAR PARK, KESWICK (PARKING CHARGE)
TIME: 2 HOURS (06A), 3 HOURS (06B) » **SATNAV**: CA12 5LE » **OS MAP**: LANDRANGER 90 » **PUB**: KESWICK » **CAFE**: KESWICK.

From the Otley Road car park, go back out on to Bank Street and turn **L**. Turn **L** on to Station Road just after the pedestrian crossing (traffic lights), and follow the road to a mini roundabout. Turn **L** into the leisure centre car park and, once in the car park, **L** again on to the old railway line, signed *Keswick Railway Footpath*. Follow this out of the car park and continue **SA** along it for around 5km.

2 At the main road, turn **L** and then **L** again shortly afterwards, towards Threlkeld. Ride into the village, taking the second **L**, signed *Blease Road Leading to Blencathra*.

3 Climb up the lane **ignoring** all turnings, until you reach the Blencathra Centre. Keep **R** and ride **SA** through a small car park on to a wide stone bridleway, signed *Skiddaw House*. Follow the obvious track up the valley. At the valley head, follow the track to the left, descend to ford the river and then climb to a bridleway T-junction.

4 Turn **L** to climb back along the western side of the valley. Tricky riding (watch the drop ...) leads through a gate to an easier track. Follow this to pass through two more gates. Turn **R** just after the second gate, through a third into a small car park.

5 Turn **L** through a gate at the far side of the car park. (A sign on the gate warns cyclists of the drainage ditches.) This track can be busy, so take care. Bear **R** at the fork and descend around switchbacks. Keep **R** at the next fork, go **SA** through the gate and turn **L** at the road. Ride to the mini roundabout and retrace your outward route.

ALTITUDE PROFILE – 06A LONSCALE FELL LOOP

SKIDDAW FOREST

Skiddaw Ho

Mungrisdale Comm
633

Cloven Stone

p113 Skiddaw Loop

Sale How
666

415

4

SADDLEBACK OR
BLENCATHRA

Little Man
865

Jenkin
Hill

715

Mine (dis)

LONSCALE FELL

Blease Fell

Middle
Tongue

804
Knowe
Crags

Gategill
Fell

3

Underscar Manor
(Hotel)

Lonscale
Derwentfolds

Blencathra
Field Centre

High Row
Fm

Threlkeld

Ormathwaite

5

Malle odd

Brundholme

Wescoe

The
Riddings

186

2

136

Latrigg
368

Brundholme
Wood

Briery

Burns Fm

Birkett
Mire

Goosewell
Fm

148

Hollin
Root

Mire
Ho

Birkett
Bank

Brigham

Fieldside

Stone
Circle

Tewet
Tarn

Shundraw

Chestnut
Hill

209

Wanthwaite

K

Moor
214

Row
End

Yew Tree
Fm

Castlerigg

Nest

Low Rigg

30

Bridge
Ho

Rakefoot

181

Sykes

357

Dale
Bottom

**06A Lonscale
Fell Loop**

359
Pike

Causeway
Foot

158

Directions – Two from Keswick – Skiddaw

➲ From Otley Road car park, go back out on to Bank Street and turn **L**. Turn **L** on to Station Road just after the pedestrian crossing (traffic lights), and follow the road to a mini roundabout.

2 Turn **R** and follow the road past houses for 300m before turning **R** on to an obvious bridleway.

3 **Ignoring** all turnings, climb to a gate leading into a car park. Turn **R** through the car park, turning **L** immediately beyond the gate at the far end. Pass through two more gates and bear **L** at the fork just after the second.

4 Climb!

5 Stick to the obvious track, climbing continuously until you reach the summit. Take a breather and then retrace your steps (at a considerably higher speed) to your car.

ALTITUDE PROFILE – 06B SKIDDAW

⫷◯▭ Making a day of it
Either of these short routes can be added into the **Skiddaw Loop** on page 113. The Lonscale Fell Loop in particular makes a great alternative start to this longer ride.

06B **Skiddaw**

NEAR SILVER POINT

Introduction

For the technically able, this is an awesome little ride. Using mainly stone-based tracks, it's also a fairly all-weather loop, although it can get a little boggy higher up. You might want to choose a different route on a sunny Sunday, as the superb track alongside Ullswater (the highlight of the ride) can get crowded with walkers. Never climbing to the high fell-tops that characterise many routes in the North Lakes, the route avoids forcing you off the bike for a long portage. Don't underestimate it or make the mistake of deciding it's an easy ride though: there's still a (very) steep climb to be conquered; and the wide stone singletrack along Ullswater that seems tantalisingly doable – and yet often proves to be a little too technical to be cleaned.

The Ride

A quick spin along the road takes you on to a bridleway through fields at Bridgend. Cross the river on to a wide stone track and head steeply uphill, climbing 200 metres in just over a kilometre. Take a breather(!) at the top and admire the views out across the valley towards Helvellyn. Cross the plateau on vague trails and pick up the fast and swoopy singletrack descent into Martindale and on to tarmac. Roll down the road to a short grassy bridleway and then on to Sandwick. A grassy bridleway just before the car park starts innocently enough, soon becoming rocky and heading downhill before turning into a mega-technical undulating trail running along the shore of Ullswater. If you can clean this, you're doing well!

ALTITUDE PROFILE

BEDA FELL

Metres

0 Km 5 10 15

ULLSWATER SINGLETRACK GRADE: ▲

TOTAL DISTANCE: 18KM/11 MILES » **TOTAL ASCENT**: 720M/2,362FT » **START/FINISH**: CAR PARK IN PATTERDALE
START GR: NY 397159 » **PARKING**: PAY AND DISPLAY IN PATTERDALE » **TIME**: 2-3 HOURS » **SATNAV**: CA11 0NW
OS MAP: LANDRANGER 90 » **PUB**: WHITE LION INN, PATTERDALE, TEL: 01768 482 214 » **CAFE**: NONE.

Directions – Ullswater Singletrack

↱ Leave Patterdale on the A592, heading south, away from Ullswater towards the Kirkstone Pass. After 1.8km, turn **L** on to a signed bridleway, just before the last house in Bridgend. If you reach a red phone box on the right, you've gone too far.

2 Follow the bridleway through gates and fields, crossing the river and meeting a wide track. Turn **R** and then sharply back **L** after a short distance to climb steeply up a wide track towards Boredale Hause.

3 After a very steep section the gradient eases as the track swings to the right and reaches a plateau. Head for the ridge on the east side of the plateau. **Ignoring** obvious tracks to the left and right, the bridleway heads **L** at a 45° angle on a vague grassy trail, before cutting back **R** and up to the ridge. As you reach the far side of the plateau, the track swings left (north-east) as it climbs up on to the ridge and turns to perfect singletrack.

4 Summiting the ridge, go **SA** over a crossroads of narrow tracks (bearing slightly to the **R** and then back **L** as you start to descend). Awesome singletrack descent into Martindale. Stick to the 'main' track all the way (anything else is a sheep track). Pick up the road at the buildings at Dale Head and follow it down the valley.

5 Turn **L** on to a grassy bridleway just before a farm and a bridge. Follow it to the road and turn **L** (**SA** in effect). Descend round a hairpin, following signs for *Sandwick*. Turn **L** immediately before the car park on to a bridleway signed *Bridleway to Patterdale*.

6 The track turns to technical singletrack which undulates along the side of Ullswater. Stick to the main obvious track and **ignore** all turnings. The track eventually widens after a final climb and becomes a well-made track.

7 Go **SA** through the gate at Side Farm and **SA** through the next gate on to tarmac. Follow the road round to the right and out to Patterdale.

⚙ Making a day of it
This route is right beside the **High Street North** ride (see page 121), and adds a little technical spice to that route.

07 Ullswater Singletrack

Section 2

Epics

Getting longer now – these loops will take a bit more time and effort. Not rides to be scared of, but definitely rides to be respected. Rather large hills and plenty of technical ground to cover mean that firstly, you're going to be out for a good few hours and secondly, you're going to have a really good time.

ROCKY TRAILS ON THE IRON KELD & LOUGHRIGG (ROUTE 13)

FINE SINGLETRACK NEAR STAINTON GROUND (ROUTE 12)

HEADING OVER GREEN QUARTER FELL

Introduction

Another classic ride in the Kentmere Valley, looping anticlockwise over into Longsleddale and back again. This route gives a great introduction to Lake District riding without having to travel into the heart of the Lakes, thus avoiding both the crowds and the journey time. The riding on the east side of the valley can feel very remote, even though it's so close to the village of Staveley. It's worth noting that this side of the valley can be quite boggy after continued rain, so choose your day carefully. Kentmere is a great area for the novice biker looking to become a bit more adventurous, or for those wanting to start and end their ride at a great cafe.

The Ride

This ride takes you to the quiet and picturesque valley of Longsleddale. Leaving Staveley on metalled roads, it's not long before a track takes you on to the open fells of Kentmere. There are many alternative bridleways in this area, but this route follows the well-worn track leading to Green Quarter. After some good singletrack the ride breaks off right on ill-defined bridleways to Longsleddale, where the vague tracks give way to a solid trail and a great downhill. Spin up the valley on tarmac and a good trail climbs over to Green Quarter, from where you'll soon find yourself in the picturesque village of Kentmere. From here it's uphill on good tracks to Whiteside End and a rest for your legs on the downhills that follow, taking you all the way back to the start.

ALTITUDE PROFILE

SLEDDALE FOREST · COCKLAW FELL · WHITESIDE END

KENTMERE & LONGSLEDDALE   GRADE: ▲

TOTAL DISTANCE: 23KM/14MILES » **TOTAL ASCENT**: 704M/2,310FT » **START/FINISH**: STAVELEY MILL YARD
START GR: SD 472982 » **PARKING**: STAVELEY MILL YARD (2-HOUR LIMIT IN THE WEEK WITHOUT PERMIT; NO RESTRICTIONS AT WEEKENDS) » **TIME**: 2-3 HOURS » **SATNAV**: LA8 9LR » **OS MAP**: LANDRANGER 90; LANDRANGER 97
PUB: EAGLE & CHILD, STAVELEY, TEL: 01539 821 320 » **CAFE**: WILF'S CAFE, STAVELEY, TEL: 01539 822 329.

↪ Turn **R** out of the car park on to Back Lane, and then **R** again at the main Kentmere road, heading north-west.

2 Turn **R** over Barley Bridge (weir), then immediately **L** to climb up Hall Lane. Continue **SA**, climbing quite steeply in parts, until you reach Park End (Park House on the map). Continue **SA** on to a farm track, which gradually opens out.

3 Follow the wall, **ignoring** bridleways on the left, until the track takes you away from the wall and through a gate. Bear **R** (*bridleway* sign) at the fork, heading north-east (the left fork is not a bridleway). The trail continues uphill on some great singletrack that feels as though it's in a shallow ravine. **Easy to miss**: as you exit the ravine, the trail forks by a cairn. Take the vague trail to the **R**.

4 Continue **SA**, heading for a gate in a wall. Go through the gate, over a footbridge and follow the trail, heading roughly east, through some fine scenery with a great sense of seclusion and remoteness.

5 Eventually a final gate leads to a descent that swings left (north) into Longsleddale. At the end of the downhill, go through the **R** of the two gates by the cottages (Valley View and Spring Cottage) on to a signed bridleway. Continue downhill and follow the track out to Wadshowe Bridge and the road. (**Note:** You can take the bridleway that turns left past the cottages to Till's Hole, but this is generally hard work and can be very boggy.)

6 Turn **L** along the road and head north to Sadgill. **Ignore** the first bridleway to Kentmere at Till's Hole (after 2km) and continue for another 800m, following the road over a bridge (the track running straight ahead is Gatescarth Pass leading to Haweswater). Once over the bridge turn **L** at a *bridleway* sign then **R** in front of the farm to another gate.

7 Climb gradually through Sadgill Wood (heading south) to a gate. Once through this gate, **ignore** the bridleway to the left and continue **SA** up the steep track in front of you (this is a good technical downhill, but unfortunately you're going up it!). The track eventually plateaus and a fun downhill (with a few gates) follows.

08 **Kentmere & Longsleddale**

8 Join the road (High Lane) and turn **L** towards Kentmere. After a gate and a fast downhill, take the first road on your **R** (goes back acutely) and descend to Low Bridge. Turn **R** towards Kentmere Church. Just before the church, turn **L** on to the bridleway (on tarmac initially) to Kentmere Hall.

9 Follow the track **SA** through the gate and round to the left, where the uphill struggle starts, albeit on good trails – so no getting off here apart from the gates! At the top, the trail swings to the right and downhill – enjoy. After short steep downhill section the track swings back left and through a gate.

10 Immediately beyond the gate, the bridleway forks. Bear **L** (do not ford the stream), for an exhilarating downhill. Follow this through Croft Head to Ullthwaite Bridge. Go over the bridge and turn **R** along the Kentmere road for an easy spin back to Wilf's for your cake and tea.

Making a day of it
Continue over the **Garburn Pass** from Kentmere (page 19).

NEAR WHITESIDE END

09 Whitbarrow Scar

22km/14 miles

Introduction

This is a two-hour-plus ride on the edge of the Lake District National Park. Passing through some beautiful, semi-natural woodland, this is a route which throws up a few surprises that will have you screaming for more!

The Ride

The route starts from Raven's Lodge, and from the moment you leave tarmac it starts to climb below White Scar. From the top, the bridleway drops down to Mill Side where we take a sharp right in the direction of Witherslack Hall School and Equestrian Centre. From here, after a brief interlude on tarmac, the route heads into the woods for a rollercoaster descent into Witherslack village. Pounding blacktop for a couple of kilometres soon sees us off-road again, this time on a challenging climb back up to Witherslack Hall. Turning left, the route follows the quiet lane to Broad Oak where another challenging climb is rewarded with a 'how-fast-can-I-go' downhill. From the end of which we join the A5074 for the ride back to the car.

ALTITUDE PROFILE

Metres — 120, 0

0 Km   2.5   5   7.5   10   12.5   15   17.5   20

YEWBARROW

TOWNSHIP ALLOTMENT

WHITBARROW SCAR   **GRADE:** ▲

TOTAL DISTANCE: 22KM/14 MILES » **TOTAL ASCENT**: 502M/1,647FT » **START/FINISH**: RAVEN'S LODGE » **START GR**: SD 463851
PARKING: ON OLD A590 AT THE HEAD OF THE LANE TO RAVEN'S LODGE » **TIME**: 2-3 HOURS » **SATNAV**: LA8 8EU
OS MAP: LANDRANGER 97 » **PUB**: GILPIN BRIDGE INN, TEL: 01539 552 206 » **CAFE**: NONE ON ROUTE.

S Ride down the lane towards the farm. As soon as you pass the farm entrance on the right, turn **L** through a gate, passing a cowshed. Continue through the next gate on to the first climb.

2 Climb through the wood, sticking to the bridleway, until it eventually tops out and exits the wood, soon joining an unmade road by a gateway. Turn **R**, heading away from the gateway. The lane soon turns to tarmac, heading downhill quite steeply and passing a farm on the left.

3 At the bottom of the hill do not continue to the road junction, but turn sharp **R** (almost back on yourself) in the direction of Beck Head.

4 After 750m, this lane turns to an unmade track by some cottages. Continue **SA**, bearing **L** through a gateway. The track climbs slightly then continues to a junction with a metalled road. Turn **R** in the direction of Witherslack Hall. Turn **L** at the hall along a track signed to *Knot Wood*.

5 Follow the track, immediately bearing **L** and ignoring the bridleway to the right. A quick descent leads to a field by some cottages. Bear **R**, away from the cottages, to a gate on the opposite side of the field. Pass through the gate and continue along the track with the wall on your left. The track then breaks out into open country and leads to a junction. Turn **R**, signposted with a blue bridleway waymarker, and bear **L** at the fork to climb to a gate in the wall.

6 From the gate, follow singletrack into the wood. The next section is one of the highlights of the route as it soon starts to descend. Turn **L** by a cairn just after a steep section of descent and continue down to the road. Turn **R**. Follow the road for 2km **ignoring** roads on the left. At a sharp left-hand bend turn **R** through a gate on to a track, signed *Bridleway, Witherslack Hall*. Climb to the hall, turning **L** through a gateway at the very top of the hill.

7 At the road, turn **L** and follow the minor road **SA** for approximately 3km, passing two roads on the left.

09 **Whitbarrow Scar**

8   After a left-hand bend, the road begins to climb. On the brow of the hill, turn **R** on to a track by an old kiln. Climb steeply towards a gate, following the track to the right at the gate. At the T-junction at the top of the hill, turn **L** and follow the bridleway through two gates on to a fast descent to Row. Join tarmac (**with care** – this is a residential area and there could be vehicles) and continue **SA** down to the A5074.

9   Turn **R** and continue for 300m. At a sharp left-hand bend, turn **R** on to a lane and climb through the village of The Howe. Descend to a crossroads and turn **R** towards Flodder Hall. After 1.5km, rejoin the A5074 and turn **R** towards Gilpin Bridge.

10   At the T-junction turn **R** past the Gilpin Bridge Inn (or stop off for a swift pint maybe?) then take the cycleway back to the old A590 and your car.

Making a day of it

The **Cartmel Fell** ride (page 13) lies to the west of this route. Linking the two would create a long but technically straightforward day out.

DESCENDING TO LIMEFITT PARK

10 Troutbeck & Jenkin Crag

20km/12 miles

Introduction

Set in the hotspot of Ambleside and the surrounding area, this is a varied and surprisingly technical ride that is great for an evening or when there are other things that must be done during the day, and makes an exciting night ride for the more adventurous. It's also a nice way of getting out from Ambleside over towards Kentmere, High Street and Garburn, if you're looking for a longer day out.

The Ride

Although the route starts with the often busy A591, a bit of road work acts as a nice warm-up as the start of the off-road terrain begins steeply. Some great little downhills lead to Town End before tarmac climbs gently to Dubbs Road. More gradual climbing leads past Dubbs Reservoir and toward the top of the speedy downhill that takes you down into Limefitt Park. Climb back up to Troutbeck and then Robin Lane for the final downhill. This can be very testing depending on whether or not you decide on the escape route or commit yourself to the rocky steps. Either way, this is one of the better downhills in the area.

TROUTBECK & JENKIN CRAG GRADE: ▲

TOTAL DISTANCE: 20KM/12 MILES » **TOTAL ASCENT**: 967M/3,173FT » **START/FINISH**: BROW HEAD FARM
START GR: NY 370045 » **PARKING**: AMBLESIDE, OR ROADSIDE PARKING AT BROW HEAD FARM » **TIME**: 2-3 HOURS
SATNAV: LA22 9LJ » **OS MAP**: LANDRANGER 90 » **PUB**: MANY CHOICES IN AMBLESIDE » **CAFE**: AMBLESIDE.

↪ From the farm head south to Rothay Bridge. Turn **L** and follow the one-way system, turning **R** to Waterhead. At Waterhead turn **R** on to the A591 following signs for *Windermere* and *Kendal*. Be careful as the road is narrow in parts and for some reason the cars seem to ignore cyclists. After 4.5km turn **L** on to Mirk Lane (shortly after signs for the *Brockhole Centre* on your right and the *Merewood Hotel* on your left).

2 Climb steeply past buildings and through woods to a road. Turn **L**. After a short distance, more track takes you steeply uphill once again.

3 At the T-junction with the road turn **R** for 700m, passing a track (bridleway) which doubles back on the right and then a bridleway on the left. Soon after a lay-by on the right, turn **R** on to a bridleway and descend towards Town End. Cross the road, heading **SA** on to a signed bridleway and descend to two footbridges (or ford the river). Head up the grass bank to the road.

4 Turn **R** and then first **L** on to Moorhowe Road, climbing steeply at first. After 2km, on a right-hand bend, turn **L** along a track with a dead end sign. This is Dubbs Road.

5 Head north, climbing pleasantly past Dubbs Reservoir and through gates for 2.5km to a T-junction with Garburn Road. Turn **L**, downhill, almost back on yourself, heading south-west. A great downhill follows. Don't get too carried away – turn **R** on to a bridleway after 600m, doubling back on yourself and passing through a gate.

6 Continue downhill, taking the next **L** (alongside the wall) and dropping through a final gate into the caravan park. Follow *bridleway* signs along the road through the centre of the park and join the main road.

7 Turn **L** and, after 200m, turn **R** on to a track just before the church, by an old water trough. Climb gently up singletrack, keeping **L** at the bridleway junction, to join the road.

10 **Troutbeck &
Jenkin Crag**

8 Turn **L** and, after a short distance, turn **R** up the road past The Old Post Office. Climb steeply for a short distance on tarmac and continue for 1.2km to a fork, **ignoring** bridleways on the left. Bear **L** (signed *Jenkin Crag*) through two gates. After the second, keep **R**, uphill, to High Skelghyll Farm. **Dismount** and walk through the farm buildings, then saddle-up for the next descent.

9 The final section past Jenkin Crag and through Skelghyll Wood is a joy. Some steep rocky sections need some commitment, as do the root-covered boulders. This is a popular walk so take care. The final steep tarmac brings you out behind the mountain rescue centre on the outskirts of Ambleside. All you need to do is find your car, a cafe or a pub.

◄◷◌ **Making a day of it**

This route makes an excellent start to several longer routes for those based in Ambleside. Link to the **Garburn Pass** (page 19), then to the **Kentmere & Longsleddale** route (page 43) and, from there, as far as you like!

THE TONGUE AND TROUTBECK PARK

ABOVE TROUTBECK

11 Ings & Winster

Introduction

A surprisingly good low-level ride on the outskirts of Staveley. If you prefer country lanes and bridleways to rocky slopes, then this is the route for you. Generally, the lanes you will encounter are only used by local traffic and are very quiet. There is very little technical off-road, although there is a short steep section just after Thornyfields and a great downhill after Birk Moss. A great introduction to 'proper' Lake District mountain biking if you've just come off the family trails at Grizedale and want a longer ride.

The Ride

From Ings, the route heads south-west to Borwick Fold before going off-road for a short section and back on to country lanes heading south-east to Crook. Then it heads south-west, taking you through an extended off-road section past Crook Hall and along trails past High House and Birk Moss. It then takes you through to Winster via the pretty hamlet of Thorny-fields. From here you climb north-east on country lanes, before a great trail leads to Lindeth Lane. This takes you on to the B5284, the only busy road, which has one short climb past the Winder-mere Golf Club before heading off north-east on country lanes back to Ings.

ALTITUDE PROFILE

BORWICK FOLD — BULMAN STRANDS — SUMMER GROVE PLANTATION

INGS & WINSTER GRADE: ▲

TOTAL DISTANCE: 23KM/14 MILES » **TOTAL ASCENT**: 670M/2,198FT » **START/FINISH**: INGS » **START GR**: SD 444987
PARKING: ROADSIDE PARKING IN INGS (PARKING MAY BE LIMITED, PARTICULARLY AT WEEKENDS); PLEASE PARK RESPONSIBLY
TIME: 2–3 HOURS » **SATNAV**: LA8 9PY » **OS MAP**: LANDRANGER 97 » **PUB**: WATERMILL INN, INGS, TEL: 01539 821 309
CAFE: WILF'S CAFE, STAVELEY, TEL: 01539 822 329.

S➔ Go **SA** up the small lane, signed *Borwick Fold*, opposite the small car park and pub in Ings. Follow this for 2km, gradually climbing to a T-junction.

2 Turn **R** and, after 200m, turn **L** on to a bridleway towards Borwick Fold. Follow the bridleway, which is vague in places, south through a field. After 500m, join the Dales Way and turn **L** along it to emerge on a country lane. Turn **R** along this, heading south-east and downhill for 2.2km to the village of Crook.

3 At the busy T-junction turn **R**, and take the first **L** on to Dobby Lane shortly afterwards. Climb to a T-junction and turn **L**. After 300m, turn **R** on to a small lane signed *Crook Hall*. At the fork, bear **R** (still signed *Crook Hall*) and, at a second fork by a cattle grid, go **SA** over the cattle grid and through a gate on the **L**.

4 Follow the wall and trail west-north-west to a T-junction with a pathway. Turn **L** and head south-west on poorly defined trails to a bridge, and then uphill to join a confluence of several routes. **Ignoring** footpaths, bear **L** then **R** (marked with a *bridleway* sign) and follow the trail for 500m to the buildings at Birk Moss. **Do not** go through the farmyard, but take the bridleway to the **L** of the buildings. Climb to a T-junction, turn **L** and head south. A great little descent, initially on a trail then vaguely across fields, leads to a junction with the Crosthwaite road.

5 Turn **R** and, after 500m, take the bridleway on the **L** that passes in front of Crook Foot, initially following the picturesque stream north-west before heading to Thornyfields. Bear **L** in front of the houses and then turn **L** behind the barn and through a gate with a *bridleway* sign. A short, sharp climb follows and, as we know, many ascents are followed by descents. This one takes you down to the A5074.

6 Turn **R**, heading towards Winster, and take the first turning on the **R** in front of the pub. (Of course you could always stop for refreshments!) Follow this uphill for 1km until it flattens out and passes Knipe Tarn. Shortly after the tarn, pass a turning on the right and start to descend – but don't go too fast because you need to turn **L** along an unsigned trail 500m after the tarn.

11 Ings & Winster

7 Follow this west for 1.6km, **ignoring** turnings, with a good downhill finish bringing you to Lindeth Lane. Turn sharp **R** and head north for 1.6km to a crossroads with the B5284. Turn **R** uphill (carefully – it can be fast and busy) for 1.5km, passing Windermere Golf Club and take the second lane on the **L** after the club (after a small tarn), heading north-east towards Borwick Fold for 2km to a T-junction.

8 Turn **L** and ride past the entrance to Yews to a T-junction. (The bridleway through Yews shown on some maps is actually a footpath, so **don't take it**.) Turn **R** to Whasdike and turn **R** on to a bridleway in front of the building. Go through a gate into a copse and continue **SA** (a footpath goes off left) on a great little bit of singletrack. Leave the copse via another gate and bear **L** round a hilly knoll to the lane that leads back to Ings. Turn **L** and retrace your route to your car.

◄◦◯ Making a day of it

Ride north to **Garburn Pass** (page 19) to create a long and fairly technical route, or south to search out some more gentle bridleways and go exploring.

12 Broughton Moor & Seathwaite 21km/13 miles

Introduction

This is a great day out. Even though the ride is only 21 kilometres in length, it feels bigger and takes a bit longer than you would think. It packs in everything for the experienced rider: good singletrack, technical climbs and storming descents.

Route finding can be a little tricky at times, as tracks can be vague or unmarked – or there can simply be a fair few to choose from – so a compass is always useful to make sure you're heading in the right direction!

The Ride

The ride starts in the forest of Broughton Moor, initially heading west on forest roads before some great singletrack bridleways lead to Stephenson Ground. From the farm, head north-west along Long Mire (not as bad as it sounds) before a storming downhill drops into Seathwaite and the Newfield Inn. A bit of tarmac spinning leads down the Dunnerdale Valley – a beautiful area, not visited by so many tourists, where a pleasant track takes you through some great countryside and Birks Wood, to come out at Birks. Push uphill for a short while before heading east, back over the Dunnerdale Fells and round Raven's Crag to what looks like a fierce uphill, but is actually very rideable. Downhills and singletrack take you back to Stephenson Ground and the start.

ALTITUDE PROFILE

320

Metres

FOX HAW

STICKLE PIKE

80

0 Km   5   10   15   20

BROUGHTON MOOR & SEATHWAITE   GRADE: ▲

TOTAL DISTANCE: 21KM/13 MILES » **TOTAL ASCENT**: 818M/2,684FT » **START/FINISH**: BROUGHTON MOOR FOREST
START GR: SD 253927 » **PARKING**: BROUGHTON MOOR FOREST CAR PARK » **TIME**: 2-4 HOURS » **SATNAV**: LA20 6AH
OS MAP: LANDRANGER 96 » **PUB**: OPTIONS IN CONISTON OR NEWFIELD INN, SEATHWAITE, TEL: 01229 716 208
CAFE: BLUEBIRD CAFE, CONISTON, TEL: 01539 441 649.

Directions – Broughton Moor & Seathwaite

➔ From the car park, head downhill (north-east) along the road for 500m and turn **L** through a gate into the forest. Descend on the forest road to a right-hand bend and start to climb.

2 **Ignore** the forest road on the left. On the brow of the climb, turn **L** on to a bridleway to descend on superb singletrack. At the junction with the forest road below, turn **L**.

3 The forest road descends to cross a concrete bridge and climbs steeply to another forest road. Turn **L** and then **R (easy to miss)** on to singletrack just after a right-hand bend. Follow this orgasmic singletrack to drop steeply to yet another forest road. Turn **R** then immediately **L** down a bridleway. Continue through the gate to the lane and turn **R**, crossing the bridge and climbing steeply to the farm (Stephenson Ground).

4 At the farm, turn **R** through a gate, signed *bridleway* and then bear **L** heading towards Seathwaite (the bridleway to the right leads to Walna Scar). Head north-west, climbing steeply alongside the wall, and follow the bridleway across the stream. Follow the track between walls by the stream, passing through a second gated wall to a 3-way junction.

5 Turn **L** and continue downhill by the wall. As the wall bears left, bear **R** at the fork (essentially **SA**). Pleasant singletrack leads through undulating terrain (trending uphill), eventually opening out and reaching two cairns. **Ignore** the track to the right and continue **SA** on to a technical and fast (or as fast as you want to make it) descent to Seathwaite and the Newfield Inn – of course it could end sooner if you come off!

6 Turn **L** along the road, following the River Duddon to the west and then south. Bear **L** at the road junction just before Hall Bridge (phone box) heading in the direction of Broughton Mills. As the road bears sharply left and uphill, turn **R** on to a bridleway running through Far Kiln Bank.

7 Follow the pleasant track through Birks Wood to Birks, turning **L** along a steep bridleway opposite the house. As the bridleway becomes vague, keep heading **SA** and east over the Dunnerdale Fells. The track can be difficult to find but offers some great singletrack. Contour around the side of the hill to the road.

12 **Broughton Moor & Seathwaite**

Note: The bridleway can be difficult to find. If you hit the road near the cattle grid, you are too far north – turn **R** and head uphill to the top of the hill and turn **L** (east) on to a signed bridleway.

8 If you managed to keep to the bridleway, you will arrive at the road at the top of the hill. Go **SA** (east) on to the signed bridleway. Follow the bridleway downhill to a crossroads with a larger track. Continue **SA** over this on to a sometimes boggy bridleway leading to a wall and then contouring around the hillside (this is Raven's Crag).

9 Follow this bridleway up the challenging climb to the crest of the ridge to meet another bridleway coming from Stainton Ground. Turn **L** and descend, following the bridleway to Jackson Ground. **Do not** go into the farm – follow the track around it to join a bridleway heading south-east and back to Stephenson Ground. From here, retrace your steps to your car or follow the optional forestry road route.

OR As you join the main forestry road, head south downhill, bearing **L** at the first junction and following the track for some way. Bear **R** at the next junction, cross a bridge and descend to a fork. Bear **L**, turn **L** again at the next junction and follow the track back to the start.

Making a day of it
Adding the **Walna Scar** ride (page 127) to this would create a nice figure-8 ride.

NEAR TILBERTHWAITE

13 Iron Keld & Loughrigg

24km/15 miles

Introduction

This is a great ride into the heart of the South Lakes, travelling among some great mountain scenery without having to gain a lot of height! Navigation is straightforward, as the route follows well waymarked bridleways at all times. In addition, the bridleways are mostly stone-based, so this is a route that can be ridden year round. There are plenty of opportunities for cafe or pub stops along the way.

The Ride

Head north from Grizedale Forest in the direction of Tarn Hows to the rocky Tarn Hows byway, which leads over to the busy Coniston/Ambleside road. More tracks lead straight up past Hodge Close Quarry and into Little Langdale via a tricky climb and long, rocky descent. Climb up the hill for a fast, and again rocky, descent into the picturesque village of Elterwater in Great Langdale Valley and take the road to climb over to Loughrigg for a fun descent down the scenic terrace. (Watch out for walkers here.) Climb back over Loughrigg and hit the road out of Skelwith Bridge to the bridleway to Iron Keld, a National Trust owned forest which has been dramatically altered recently due to harvesting. A rocky but fast descent leads us to rejoin the Tarn Hows byway for the return stretch to the car park at High Cross.

ALTITUDE PROFILE

IRON KELD & LOUGHRIGG — **GRADE:** ▲

TOTAL DISTANCE: 24KM/15 MILES » **TOTAL ASCENT**: 885M/2,904FT » **START/FINISH**: HIGH CROSS, GRIZEDALE FOREST
START GR: SD 332986 » **PARKING**: HIGH CROSS CAR PARK » **TIME**: 2.5-4 HOURS » **SATNAV**: LA22 0PW
OS MAP: LANDRANGER 90; LANDRANGER 96 OR 97 » **PUB**: HAWKSHEAD OR CONISTON » **CAFE**: HAWKSHEAD OR CONISTON.

13 **Iron Keld & Loughrigg**

Directions – Iron Keld & Loughrigg

S→ Exit the car park and go **SA** over the main road on to the minor road opposite, heading for Tarn Hows. After 1.5km, drop sharply downhill and turn **L** on to a wide byway immediately after a road junction on the right. Pass behind the cottage (*Borwick Lodge* is signposted on the right).

2 Follow the byway for approx. 2.8km, **ignoring** all turnings, to join a metalled track. Follow it to the main Coniston/Ambleside road.

3 Cross the road and continue **SA** on the singletrack lane opposite. Climb steeply and then descend to the farm at High Oxen Fell. Go **SA** through a gate on to a bridleway as tarmac ends. Climb to another gate and then descend to a third at Hodge Close. Please ensure the gates are all closed behind you.

4 At the T-junction with a metalled lane, turn **L** and descend around corners through buildings. Directly opposite the last cottage on the left, turn **R** on to a track through a gate. Descend to a long right-hand bend, turning **L** to descend a rocky (slate) track in a gully immediately beyond the bend (**ignoring** the first track on the left, which stays high). Drop into the woods, cross a stream and climb a short hill, to a T-junction. Turn **L**, continuing **SA** as the track levels out.

5 Keep going to High Tilberthwaite Farm. At the farm, continue into the farmyard (**walk** while in the yard) and turn sharp **R** through a gate. Follow the rocky track for 1.5km over some challenging terrain with great views of the mountains. After descending to a second gate, continue **SA**, **ignoring** the track coming in from the right. Drop to a metalled road and then to a T-junction with the road which is at the foot of Wrynose Pass.

6 Turn **R**, following the lane for 1km, continuing **SA** at the junction and climbing to the top of the hill. Turn **L** up a narrow lane to Dale End Farm. The road gives way to track as it passes the farm and descends to a gate. Continue **SA** past the gate (**ignore** the track to the left), join tarmac and descend to a T-junction. Turn **L** to Elterwater.

7 Immediately beyond the green in Elterwater, fork **L** (between the pub and the postbox) and ride to a crossroads at the main road. Go **SA** on to the lane opposite to start the climb to Loughrigg. After 500m, turn **R** at the T-junction and continue to climb. The pain is only short-lived and you soon reach a T-junction.

OR Turn **R** to descend towards Loughrigg Tarn. Unfortunately there's no legal right of way for MTBs close to the tarn, so stick to the road. Take the second road on the **R** (after 1.7km), passing the tarn on your left and drop down a very steep hill to Skelwith Bridge. **Take great care**, this road really is steep and narrow. Watch out for cars and keep your speed down! Turn **R** to rejoin the main route at **11**.

8 At the T-junction turn **L**, quickly turning **R** on to a bridleway by a sign on the wall for *Rydal*. Follow this scenic trail (avoiding walkers where possible). It is not technical but can be narrow in places, so please be courteous to other users. Arriving at the shore of Rydal Water (a great place for a swim on a hot day), the bridleway sinks beneath the water. Look for the obvious rock step – the shoreline is shallow enough to cycle through and good fun for onlookers when you hit submerged boulders! Alternatively, you can take a higher route on a permissive bridleway via the caves (less wet). Continue along the obvious route to Pelter Bridge. **Don't** go over the bridge, but turn **R** along the road.

9 After 1.5km turn **R** on to a bridleway. Climb to Brow Head Farm and follow the obvious track **SA** as it heads south-west and downhill to skirt Ivy Crag.

10 Follow the bridleway round to the **R** to reach a T-junction with the road, beside a postbox in a wall. Turn **R**, then immediately **L** and descend steeply to join the main road at Skelwith Bridge.

11 Go **SA** over the road junction on to the A593 towards Coniston. Climb for 1.2km until the road starts to descend and turn **L** on to a signed bridleway.

12 Tricky climbing with fantastic views all around. After 1km go through a gap in the wall, with the buildings of Low Arnside just ahead. Turn immediately **L** (and uphill), following bridleway signs. The rewarding downhill comes 800m later through a gate into Iron Keld plantation. (**Ignore** the track off to the left at the gate.) Descend to the gate which opens on to your earlier route.

13 Turn **L** and retrace your steps to the road. Turn **R**, climb Hawkshead Hill and follow the road to the car park at High Cross.

Introduction

While all other areas of the Lakes will be jam packed with tourists, walkers and fellow mountain bikers, this is an area where you will find solitude, 'far from the madding crowd'. On a clear day there are fabulous views across Burnmoor Tarn and Eskdale Fell, with the Scafell range beyond. This ride offers everything for the enthusiastic mountain biker: forest bridleways, grinding uphills on good tracks, great singletrack and storming descents – it really is one of the better rides in the area. The route gains little height but the open fells can be very exposed to the wind, the paths can be vague and, after rain, certain areas can be boggy. Navigation skills would be useful if you don't know the area.

The Ride

Starting at the bottom of Hardknott Pass – which is said to be the steepest road in the UK – an easy bridleway follows the River Esk on its southern bank. After a short road section past Eskdale Outward Bound Centre, head north-east up the Miterdale Valley. A scenic trail through woodland on good bridleways leads to the climb from Bakerstead, where poor trails through the wood lead to a great ascent on to Tongue Moor and over to Burnmoor Tarn. Join the old 'Coffin Road', an old road along which the dead were taken from Wasdale to be buried at the church in Boot. Pass Burnmoor Tarn on open fell, which eventually becomes a superb technical singletrack descent into the village of Boot. Follow the road back to the start, stopping at the Wool-pack Inn for some light refreshment.

ALTITUDE PROFILE

TONGUE MOOR

MITERDALE & ESKDALE **GRADE:** ▲

TOTAL DISTANCE: 26KM/16 MILES » **TOTAL ASCENT**: 723M/2,372FT » **START/FINISH**: START OF HARDKNOTT PASS
START GR: NY 212011 » **PARKING**: LAY-BY AT THE START OF HARDKNOTT PASS » **TIME**: 3–5 HOURS » **SATNAV**: CA19 1TH
OS MAP: LANDRANGER 89; LANDRANGER 96 » **PUB**: WOOLPACK INN, ESKDALE, TEL: 01946 723 230
CAFE: SEVERAL IN CONISTON.

14 **Miterdale & Eskdale**

Directions – Miterdale & Eskdale

⟳ From the lay-by, head downhill on the road for 1km. Just before Whahouse Bridge, turn **L** on to a bridleway and follow this along the left bank of the River Esk. **Please walk** through the yard at Penny Hill Farm.

2 Just beyond Penny Hill Farm, turn **L** immediately before Doctor Bridge to follow the bridleway to Low Birker. Pleasant riding leads to the road. Turn **R**, and then keep **L** by the King George IV pub.

3 Follow the road past the Outward Bound Centre and through Eskdale Green (stopping for any supplies at Eskdale Stores). Turn **R** just beyond a left-hand turn to the train station and by a school sign on to what looks like a private drive. Follow it past the school. The road turns to track and crosses a bridge. Bear **R** on good trails, following a bridleway to the farm at Low Place.

4 Continue on the left-hand bank of the river to Miterdale Head, where the bridleway can be seen going through a large gap made by the two forests. Follow the poor bridleway steeply uphill.

5 The bridleway is vague to non-existent in places. Keep heading roughly **SA** and north-east, aiming for gates through walls. As you reach the highest point on Tongue Moor, the fells are laid out before you, with Burnmoor Tarn centre stage. Follow some great singletrack to the eventual confluence of paths from Illgill Head and the 'Coffin Road' from Wasdale.

Note: There are often paths better than the bridleway that lead to this intersection, so you may find yourself higher up the fell than expected. In clear conditions you can see the 'Coffin Road' and correct your mistake. In bad weather, keep your map and compass handy.

6 Turn **R** along the bridleway heading for Burnmoor Tarn. The track skirts around the edge of the tarn – good for cooling the feet on hotter days – and then over Bulatt Bridge. A little further on the path divides. Continue **SA** along the bridleway (a footpath bears right to Burnmoor Lodge while another bears left to a footbridge in the distance).

7 The trail is now a bit lumpy bumpy until it passes an old ruin on the right at Eller How and turns to decidedly technical downhill singletrack, which is an absolute joy. Part way down the track you have a choice of two gates, turn **R** (signed *Boot* in faded paint on the wall) and continue to Boot.

8 At the main road, turn **L** and follow the road to your car. If you have a little energy left, you can always test yourself on the road going over Hardknott Pass!

Making a day of it

Keep riding north from the top of this ride to Wasdale Head and there are bridleways running over the Sty Head and Black Sail passes. Proper 'old school' mountain biking (i.e. involving carrying!), they'll turn the day into a long one ...

15 Grizedale Loop

20km/12 miles

Introduction

Grizedale is one of the biggest forests in the Lake District and while it may lack the height of Whinlatter it makes up for it with the sheer variety of trails on offer. This route is an excellent way to get to know the forest and takes in some of the best descents without losing too much height in the process. Be under no illusion though, the climbs are frequent and some are quite technical, which adds to the interest. This is a route that can be ridden at any time of year.

The Ride

The route starts from Moor Top car park and heads west into the forest. We will then work our way south down the western side of Grizedale, enjoying spectacular views over Coniston Water and Coniston Old Man. After crossing Parkamoor, we descend to Satterthwaite village to cross over into the eastern side of the forest. Climbing steeply out of the village, the trails take us on a roller-coaster of a ride north, eventually arriving back at Moor Top.

ALTITUDE PROFILE

MONK CONISTON MOOR — HEALD BROW PASTURE — GREAT WOOD

Metres: 310 / 78

0 Km   5   10   15   20

GRIZEDALE LOOP
GRADE ▲

TOTAL DISTANCE: 20KM/12 MILES » **TOTAL ASCENT**: 657M/2,156FT » **START/FINISH**: MOOR TOP, GRIZEDALE FOREST
START GR: SD 343965 » **PARKING**: MOOR TOP CAR PARK » **TIME**: 2-3 HOURS » **SATNAV**: LA22 0QQ
OS MAP: LANDRANGER 96 OR 97 » **PUB**: HAWKSHEAD OR CONISTON » **CAFE**: HAWKSHEAD OR CONISTON.

Directions – Grizedale Loop

⮕ From Moor Top car park, head straight into the forest bearing **R** at each of the first two junctions. The forest road climbs slightly to reach a fork where we bear **L** and continue to climb gently. Follow this forest road around the right-hand bend to reach another fork; bear **L** again to start descending. Continue **SA** at the bottom of the hill to take the second forest road on the **R**, which can be seen climbing quite steeply away from us.

2 Climb the steep track until you reach an overgrown crossroads (the forest road turns sharp right; there is a footpath on the left with a marker post). Continue **SA** down a short, now singletrack, descent. We very soon pop out on to another forest road; continue **SA**, then at the fork bear **L**. This can be quite overgrown and easily missed especially as you're descending. Continue down the hill to join another forest road; turn **L**.

3 The forest road now climbs gently; bear **R** at the next two junctions. Stay on this forest road until you reach a large off-set crossroads where we bear around to the **R** and continue to gently climb until we reach a bridleway joining from the **R** (signpost). This is the start of Lawson Park descent. Turn on to the bridleway and enjoy a great descent to reach a gate at Lawson Park. Go through the gate and turn **L** down the forest road (we're not doing the full descent today). After 300m or so turn **L** (on to a forest road – **ignore** the minor farm track just prior). Pass the single bar gate on the right to then start climbing back up.

4 Follow the forest road all the way to the top and a T-junction. Turn **R** and follow this briefly to a left-hand bend and a bridleway on the **R**, signposted *Parkamoor*. Leave the forest road to follow the bridleway, which eventually brings us to a gate out on to Parkamoor. Closing the gate behind us, follow the well-defined bridleway, taking time to enjoy the views over Coniston and the Lakeland Fells.

5 After no doubt taking a few photos, continue to follow the bridleway, descending to a gate. Continue through the gate on the bridleway to another gate at Low Parkamoor. Pass the building to descend the stoney track to another gate. Pass through the gate and over the stream to climb the steep grassy track to join the main Grizedale/Nibthwaite track. Turn sharp **L** back in the direction of the forest. Follow this wide farm track all the way back to the forest boundary gate.

15 **Grizedale Loop**

6 From here we follow a series of descents known locally as 'The 3 Witches' (on Strava as 'Grandad, Dad and Dentist'). You'll cross a forest road three times on the way down. At the third crossing the bridleway drops to cross a stream then climbs quite steeply to a gate. This is start of the final descent to the road and a small car park near Satterthwaite village.

7 After that exhilarating descent and reaching the road with everything still intact, turn **L** in the direction of Satterthwaite. Ride through village taking the first **R** after the church to climb a narrow lane between the houses. At the T-junction turn **R** and climb this steep lane to a white house at the top opposite a bridleway. Turn **R** on to the bridleway to climb back into the forest.

8 The bridleway is quite technical and challenging in places but eventually joins a forest road; we cross the forest road and continue following the now singletrack bridleway. After another couple of techy sections and very brief descent we pop out on the forest road again. Cross straight over to continue following the bridleway. This is the top of Great Wood descent which starts nice and easy, crossing a stream to immediately climb sharply (be in the right gear) before dropping again, this time increasingly steep with a drop or two, eventually popping out at a car park on a minor road. Gnarrrr!

9 Join the minor road and turn **L**. Climb the steep little hill (ignore a bridleway on the right) to reach a car park on the **L**. Turn in here and pick up the bridleway again which climbs sharply and can be quite slippery in the wet (which it usually is …). The bridleway levels out into singletrack but only briefly … time to dig deep and grind our way up making the most of the flatter section over the stream to rest (unless of course you're on an ebike). The trail soon pops out on to forest road where we turn **R**.

10 Follow this forest road up a gentle hill to the next junction on a left-hand bend. Turn **R** to pick up another bridleway. The forest road soon gives way to a fun stretch of singletrack which you could be forgiven for thinking is a trail centre; however, it is a bridleway so expect people travelling in both directions! The trail ends with a short sharp climb to join a forest road where we turn **R** to head gently downhill towards 'the Fox'.

11 We soon reach a large open junction, which is watched over by 'the Fox'. Bear **R** then immediately **L** to pick up the singletrack bridleway (signpost). A short descent through dense forest brings us out on to another forest road. Bear **L** to climb the gentle hill (*bridleway* signpost). Follow this forest road all the way to a T-junction and turn **R**. Follow this downhill to a gate and the main valley road. Join the road turning **R** and then first **L** back in to Moor Top car park.

◀▭▭▭ Making a day of it
Head north-east to link up with **Claife Heights** (page 9), or head south-west to join the **Blawith Loop** (page 5).

Section 3

Enduros

Now we're talking. Pack your sarnies and your chain lube. These are big, tough rides (for big, tough riders?) that'll probably take you all day. They're challenging routes for fit and experienced mountain bikers – you know – proper riding. Riding where you might describe the route as 'a bit of a beast'.

DROPPING DOWN PAST CASTLE CRAG ON THE BORROWDALE BASH (ROUTE 17)

HEADING NORTH FROM HELVELLYN SUMMIT (ROUTE 16) © JAMES VINCENT

PEDAL ASSIST UP LOWER MAN © JAMES VINCENT

Introduction

Helvellyn is the highest mountain in England that you can legally ride on a bike. (Whether or not you do actually ride is down to you!) So be prepared for lots of climbing, big views and a huge descent. This route has lots of choices: start by either heading north along Ullswater and approaching White Side via Great Dodd, or take the shorter route via Keppel Cove. From White Side either continue on to summit Helvellyn then follow the crazily rocky descent to Grisedale Tarn (only pick this one if you're good!) or return to Glenridding via the main track or Sticks Pass.

The Ride

Warm up on tarmac, climbing away from Ullswater. Climb on (mostly) surprisingly gentle grassy tracks up Great Dodd. Then head south, admiring the view, to the descent of your choice. First is Sticks Pass – technical singletrack followed by a steep rocky section. Second, the main track to Glenridding – fast, loose and fun – watch out for walkers. Third, take on Helvellyn. The alternative start from Glenridding is the quickest route up Helvellyn via the zigzags. If you're on an ebike it will be rideable all the way to Lower Man where you finally may be forced to walk the last few hundred metres or so.

Note: This is not a particularly all-weather route as some areas get boggy. The ride is graded red for dry conditions with a finish down the Keppel Cove descent. In the wet, or if you take the Sticks Pass or Grisedale descents, it definitely becomes a black route.

Warning: This is a high mountain – the weather can be bad and visibility poor. Take a map and compass, know what you're doing and go easy on the descents. It's also popular with walkers – lots of people to crash into. **Take care!**

ALTITUDE PROFILE

950 | GREAT DODD | HELVELLYN

Metres

145 | 0 Km | 5 | 10 | 15 | 20 | 25

HELVELLYN   GRADE: ▲ » ▲

TOTAL DISTANCE: 30KM/19 MILES » **TOTAL ASCENT:** 1,273M/4,177FT » **START/FINISH:** GLENRIDDING
START GR: NY 387169 » **PARKING:** GLENRIDDING (PAY & DISPLAY) » **TIME:** 4–6 HOURS » **SATNAV:** CA11 0PB
OS MAP: LANDRANGER 90 » **PUB:** GLENRIDDING » **CAFE:** GLENRIDDING.

Directions – Helvellyn

➲ Head north out of Glenridding on the A592 along the shore of Ullswater, heading for Pooley Bridge. Turn **L** after 3.8km, signed to *Dockray*. Once in Dockray, turn **L** just after the bridge, up the lane signed to *High Row*. At the T-junction, go **SA** over the road and through a gate on to a wide dirt track.

2 Just after crossing a ford, turn **L** (immediately beyond an old fence), on to vague grassy singletrack, which soon becomes more defined. Start to climb. See that big rounded hill ahead of you? That's where you're going. The track is vague and boggy in places. Upon reaching a small rocky summit (unfortunately a false one!), bear **R** and climb steeply.

3 Just before the summit of Great Dodd, the bridleway heads off **R** to join an obvious track. Turn back **L** along it, contouring back along the hillside and up on to the ridge on the other side of the summit. Don't worry if you miss the track and reach the top of the hill, go **SA** over the summit on the obvious path (not a bridleway) and you'll soon rejoin the bridleway.

4 From here, keep going roughly **SA** and south along the ridge. Bear **L** at the fork to run along the left-hand side of the ridge before climbing Stybarrow Dodd and descending fast to a bridleway crossroads.

OR Turn **L** at the crossroads to descend Sticks Pass. Follow the obvious technical singletrack to descend to the plateau, and bear to the **R** along its far side, heading for the lowest point. The track becomes more defined and soon becomes very rocky and steep. Descend to a T-junction and turn **L** to continue down the valley to Glenridding.

5 Continue **SA** over the crossroads and climb (carry) up Raise. Go **SA** over the summit and descend to a junction. From here either follow the main route to summit Helvellyn, or follow the optional route heading east back to Glenridding (reversing the route from the Alternative Start).

16 **Helvellyn**

p35 Ullswater Singletrack

> **OR** Turn sharp **L** back on yourself along a wide track. Zigzag down the fast and loose descent, always keeping to the main track and heading down the valley. Turn **L** (keep going **SA**, really) at the T-junction and continue to YHA Helvellyn. Go through the gates, continue to tarmac and keep descending to Glenridding.

6 After topping a minor summit, the bridleway descends briefly before the final climb up Lower Man and onto the main Helvellyn ridge. Take great care with navigation here if visibility is poor, we don't want to start descending towards Thirlmere! From Lower Man it's an easy pedal over to the summit trig point of Helvellyn.

7 There are quite a few options to descend Helvellyn and this route follows one of the more challenging (the easiest way down is back the way we came up). If you've chosen the challenging option, continue southwards along the summit ridge until you reach the stone shelter; bear **R** here and start to descend. At the next fork, bear **L** on the higher bridleway towards Nethermost Pike. The bridleway actually stays just below the summits of Nethermost Pike, High Crag and Dollywaggon Pike, and is a well-defined path.

8 After circumnavigating Dollywaggon Pike we reach a metal post, bear **L**. After just a few metres we start the descent down to Grisedale Tarn. This is a very technical, steep descent and should only be attempted by experienced mountain bikers. It features large 'stone-pitching' down to the tarn and has some very large water bars built across the path, so take care!

9 The bridleway eventually eases; it doesn't actually go all the way to the edge of tarn but remains higher and continues in an easterly direction down Grisedale Valley. From the outset, the bridleway features natural, technical rocky outcrops which seasoned mountain bikers will love, occasionally pausing at different trail features to work out where the best lines are to enable a clean descent.

10 After some enjoyable technical riding we eventually reach the Outward Bound hut, Ruthwaite Lodge. The bridleway continues down towards two footbridges, we're heading for the second one (the one farthest away). Cross the bridge and continue to follow the well-defined stony track. After a couple more technical sections the track finally eases to give an easy spin following the river down the valley. Upon reaching tarmac continue **SA** at the *bridleway* sign. Follow this lane down past playing fields on the right to eventually join the main road (A592). Turn **L** to return to Glenridding and the car park.

Exit the car park and turn **L** up Greenside Road. Keep following the road as it bears **R** at Gillside Farm then bear **L** to join the track up to YHA Helvellyn (signposted *Except for access*). After reaching YHA Helvellyn continue **SA** up the Greenside Mine track, passing the buildings. Bear **R** at the sign *Brown Cove*, *Whiteside Bank* and *Sticks Pass*. Remain on this well-defined track as it makes its way up the valley alongside Glenridding Beck. After climbing for a while, we finally reach a fork; bear **R** as indicated by the small bridleway arrow. This is the start of the zigzags. Climb the occasionally quite steep bridleway all the way to the ridge. Once at the top bear **L** in a southerly direction towards Helvellyn.

Making a day of it

The **Ullswater Singletrack** (page 35) loop is only a short distance south from Glenridding, and would add an excellent couple of hours to your day.

THE OLD COACH ROAD NEAR DOCKRAY © JAMES VINCENT

GREAT RIDING ABOVE DERWENT WATER

17 Borrowdale Bash

27km/17 miles

Introduction

This is another popular loop for mountain bikers in the northern half of the Lakes. Starting from Keswick, this is a truly all-weather loop with no bogs, on which you'd have to be pretty unlucky to get lost. It's a strange route, with a lot of road work and some lovely easy trails with great views, which would make a great blue grade ride (follow the optional route for a great beginners' ride), but then there are some serious descents, massive road climbs and some technical bits of singletrack thrown in, which boost the route up to a black grade. So it's technical but easy, smooth yet rocky.

The Ride

Take care leaving Keswick – the road down Borrowdale can be busy. A tarmac lane soon leads off to the left, climbing up (and up) past some great viewpoints to Watendlath. Ford the stream and tackle the steep and rocky climb (it is doable) leading up to the top of the first of the route's descents. Drop your saddle (well, I would) and sketch your way down to Rosthwaite. Awesome! Round the end of the valley on the road, grind your way up the beginning of the Honister Pass and turn back on yourself for a fast, open descent, technical single-track and then a tyre-ripping slate descent into the woods at Grange. A bit of road and a technical climb lead to some easy undulating singletrack along the western side of Borrowdale, with some lovely views out over Derwent Water. The road leads back to Keswick.

ALTITUDE PROFILE

BRUND FELL

HONISTER PASS

Metres

330

80

0 Km   5   10   15   20   25

BORROWDALE BASH GRADE: ▲

TOTAL DISTANCE: 27KM/17 MILES » **TOTAL ASCENT**: 950M/3,117FT » **START/FINISH**: KESWICK TOWN CENTRE
START GR: NY 264235 » **PARKING**: KESWICK (PAY & DISPLAY) » **TIME**: 3-5 HOURS » **SATNAV**: CA12 5DN
OS MAP: LANDRANGER 89 OR 90 » **PUB**: IN VIRTUALLY EVERY VILLAGE ALONG THE ROUTE
CAFE: IN VIRTUALLY EVERY VILLAGE ALONG THE ROUTE.

17 **Borrowdale Bash**

Directions – Borrowdale Bash

⊙→ Follow signs out of Keswick for *Borrowdale*, following the B5289 south down the valley.

2 After 3km, turn **L** up a dead-end road, signed *Watendlath,* and climb steeply.

> **OR** Continue on the B5289 for just over 6km and turn **R** over a double-arch stone bridge, signed *Grange*. Pick up the route again at **7**.

3 Follow the road to its end in Watendlath and bear **R** where the road splits. Cross the river, go through the gate and keep **R**, heading for the steep stone climb ahead (signed *Bridleway to Rosthwaite*). Climb steeply and follow the track **SA** over the top on to a steep and very rocky descent. Stick to the main track, **ignoring** turnings until the track swings to the left and flattens slightly by a gate in a wall, signed *Bridleway, Rosthwaite*.

4 Follow the track down, through a gate to tarmac and turn **R** over a bridge to the main road. Turn **L**. Go through Seatoller and climb very steeply up the start of the Honister Pass. About 300m after a cattle grid, turn sharp **R** on to an obvious track signed *Bridleway*.

5 **Easy to miss:** Drop back down towards the valley for just over 1km, looking out for a narrow trail forking **L** opposite a low wooden sign, signed *Bridleway: Grange*. If you reach some small woods with a gate in the middle, you've gone too far. Continue **SA** through a gate and follow the obvious and technical singletrack across bridges, ignoring all turnings, to a fast rocky descent down into the woods.

6 Stick to the main track. Cross a bridge as the track flattens and follow it through the woods to the river. Turn **L** at the river and pick up a good track through a campsite. Follow this to the road, turn **R** and ride into Grange. Turn **L**.

7 Follow the road out of Grange for just over 1km to the houses on your left at Manesty. Just past the house and immediately beyond a small wall that juts out towards the road, turn **L** on to the bridleway (with the large rock in the middle of the track).

8 Climb steeply to a fork by a small cairn and bear **R**, heading for the uphill edge of the woods to your right. Technical singletrack. Keep going **SA** as you leave the woods behind on to an easy and initially grassy track which soon becomes a more obvious track. Follow this as it drops down to the road by a parking bay. After 10m, on the other side of the bay, keep **L** and pick up the bridleway again.

9 At the road, turn **L** (**SA** in effect) and go round two hairpins. Bear **R** at the next junction, following signs for *Keswick*.

10 In the village of Portinscale, turn **R** just past the Chalet Tearooms and Restaurant on the left. Ride to the end of the road and cross the footbridge. Turn **R** at the T-junction with the main road and ride into Keswick.

◄⊙⊙ Making a day of it

This ride uses most of the bridleways in the valley. You could try following the Honister Pass up for a very technical descent down towards Buttermere, but you'd have to ride back up again ...

FAST AND ROCKY DESCENT TO ESTHWAITE

18 Grizedale & Esthwaite 30km/19 miles

Introduction

This is one of our favourite rides in the forest, as it has everything: technical climbs, singletrack and technical downhill. You will not be disappointed. There's even a bit of tarmac for the hardened roadie! This route will certainly change your views on the forest, if you thought it was only forestry roads for novice riders. There are 1,100 metres of ascent in the route, so, even though most of the uphill is on forestry roads and tarmac, be prepared for tired legs. As ever, the views of the mountains are spectacular, with Wetherlam and Coniston Old Man being of great prominence.

The Ride

The route circumnavigates the forest in a clockwise direction. It starts with forestry roads and singletrack to 'the Fox' before great trails take you over to Esthwaite. Undulating tarmac takes you to the next bridleway, with more stunning downhill to the road at Long Slack. After all the downhills comes an uphill stretch of tarmac. The next bridleway goes through a woodyard before climbing steeply on to Satterthwaite via the downhill at Breasty Haw. It crosses over to the west side of Grizedale and climbs, mainly on forest roads, before one of the best downhills in the forest, Lawson Park, and of course the climb back, before a final technical downhill and a saunter back to Moor Top.

GRIZEDALE & ESTHWAITE GRADE:

TOTAL DISTANCE: 30KM/19 MILES » **TOTAL ASCENT**: 1,100M/3,609FT » **START/FINISH**: MOOR TOP, GRIZEDALE FOREST
START GR: SD 343965 » **PARKING**: MOOR TOP CAR PARK » **TIME**: 3–5 HOURS » **SATNAV**: LA22 0QQ
OS MAP: LANDRANGER 96 OR 97 » **PUB**: THE EAGLES HEAD, SATTERTHWAITE, TEL: 01229 860 237
CAFE: GRIZEDALE VISITOR CENTRE, TEL: 03000 674 495.

Directions – Grizedale & Esthwaite

S➤ Turn **R** along the main road from the Moor Top car park. Within 50m, turn **L** on to a forest road and then turn **L** again at the next junction, heading east. Follow the forest road as it swings south, and then, on a sharp left-hand bend, turn **R** on to a bridleway. Follow this to a second forest road and turn **L**. ('The Fox' is off to the right if you want to have a look.)

2 After the initial rise, this track gives a fine downhill that is not without technical interest. Continue to the road.

3 Turn **R** along the road, climbing steeply south. **Easy to miss:** after 1.7km, pass a bridleway on the right, descend steeply and, as the forest opens out, turn **L** on to a bridleway signed *Long Slack*. Testing climbing to a gate. Go through the gate and follow the track round to the right. Fork **L** at the junction of two gates (marked with a *bridleway* sign).

4 Continue to climb, going **SA** over the forest road and climb for a short distance, before a great technical downhill. At the road, turn **R** and head south-south-east. Follow the road for 2.3km, climbing steeply in places.

5 Just after the *Graythwaite* sign, turn **R** at Black Brows Close (sawmill) and follow the bridleway through the sawmill yard. This is a working yard so **please take care!** As the track splits, fork **R** and climb very steeply to Hazel Seat Wood and a rewarding downhill.

6 At the forest road, go **SA** (slightly **R**), following *bridleway* signs. Within 50m, turn **R** through a deer gate on to a bridleway signed *Low Dale Park*. Technical singletrack leads to another deer gate. Go through this, through another gate and follow the bridleway down to Low Dale Park Farm and a metalled road which leads through the farm buildings.

7 Turn **L** at the T-junction with the road, then, after 100m, turn **R** on to another bridleway and either be brave and get wet fording the stream or use the footbridge and stay dry.

8 The bridleway heads uphill before it joins a forest road. (Although the bridleway continues straight ahead on the other side of the forest road and looks like a short-cut on the map, it is not.) Turn **L** (south) along the forest road and take the next **R** (heading north) back on yourself.

18 **Grizedale & Esthwaite**

9 Continue **SA** along this forest track, **ignoring** turnings, for about 500m and bear **R** at the fork (a bridleway runs off left). **Ignore** the next forest road on the right and continue **SA**, **ignoring** turnings for approximately 2km, to Breasty Haw (best name in the forest, although nothing to see). Fork **L** at the junction and, after 100m, turn **L** on to a bridleway (there is a signed bridleway to the right here), heading south-west. Join a metalled road that leads to a T-junction with the road through Satterthwaite.

10 Turn **R**, then quickly **L** on to a signed bridleway, heading west-north-west on a partially metalled road to a gate. Just before entering the forest, go through another gate to a T-junction and turn **L**.

11 At the fork, bear **R** uphill and follow the track as it curves back **L** (west) over a stream. Still climbing, bear **L** at the next fork. Continue **SA** on the forest road, **ignoring** a forest road on the left. At a major fork, bear **L** and continue to a crossroads with a *bridleway* sign. Turn **R**, still heading uphill (north) and bear **L** at the next junction. Continue **SA** for 2km, **ignoring** forest roads on the right and left, a bridleway to Parkamoor on the left and then another forest road on the left before eventually turning **L** on to a bridleway as the hill levels out to a plateau.

12 Now it's downhill for the next 2.5km so enjoy! At the buildings at Lawson Park, keep **R** on a gated track to join a metalled road on the east shore of Coniston Water. Turn **R** (heading north) for 500m and turn **R** on to a bridleway at Bank Ground, signed *Satterthwaite/Grizedale*. Attack the uphill boulder field (impressive if you can ride the first section) and, with tired legs, join another forest road, turning **R**.

13 Pass another forest road on the left and bear **L** at the fork. As the forest road bears to the right after 50m, go **SA** on to a bridleway for a stunning downhill. Join a forest road and turn **L**, **ignoring** all turnings for a 3km undulating amble back to Moor Top.

◄◯◯ Making a day of it

Explore the forest! We've suggested two other routes in the area (pages 5 and 9), but it's full of great trails that can be linked in any way you fancy. Also check out the **Grizedale Loop** on page 85.

CHARLIE SMITH AND DAVE BALSHAW ROUND LONSCALE FELL

19 Skiddaw Loop

44km/27 miles

Introduction

The bridleways around Skiddaw have long been popular with mountain bikers, and for good reason. They manage to strike a nice balance between being too hard for the less experienced and too boring for the pros. This loop takes in the popular trails and combines them with some less-used trails to form a loop with the least amount of road work possible. There are some great views, and parts of the ride have a real wilderness feel to them. You'll need to watch out in the wet, as some of the more technical sections get very slippery, and you should take a map and compass in bad weather, but otherwise this is a relatively all-weather route.

The Ride

The fantastic bridleway clinging to the side of Lonscale Fell is technical in places, slippery in the wet, and the big drop can put people off ... but it's fun and leads to Skiddaw House, from where the route descends a rutted and lumpy bridleway to Mosedale. The terrain eases and speeds increase as you reach a track and then tarmac. A stone track heads west from Calebreck over bleak fells and through old mine works. A fast, grassy descent leads to Fell Side and a short tarmac spin gives way to a green lane and another fast and grassy descent. More road work passes pink- (or is it salmon?), straw- and peppermint-coloured houses before reaching the steep track up past the atmospheric Whitewater Dash waterfall. A straight-line descent and short climb lead back to Skiddaw House and the outward route.

ALTITUDE PROFILE

490

Metres

180

0 Km   10   20   30   40

SKIDDAW HOUSE

DEER HILLS

WHITEWATER DASH

SKIDDAW LOOP

GRADE: ▲

TOTAL DISTANCE: 44KM/27 MILES » **TOTAL ASCENT**: 1,250M/4,101 FT » **START/FINISH**: NORTH OF LATRIGG, NEAR KESWICK
START GR: NY 281254 » **PARKING**: UNDERSKIDDAW CAR PARK » **TIME**: 4–6 HOURS » **SATNAV**: CA12 4PH
OS MAP: LANDRANGER 90 » **PUB**: KESWICK » **CAFE**: BRING SANDWICHES.

Directions – Skiddaw Loop

➲ Leave the car park through the gate at the end farthest from the road, immediately turning **L**. Go **SA** through the next gate and bear **R** as the track forks just after a third gate. Follow the obvious track as it contours around the side of Lonscale Fell.

2 As the track leaves the hillside, keep going **SA** up the head of the valley. **Ignore** the turning to the right just after the little ruined hut.

3 Stick to the obvious track until you reach Skiddaw House, passing alongside the wall in front of the building. As the wall ends, turn sharp **R**, heading downhill alongside another wall.

4 Follow the track (vague in places) along the left-hand side of the valley, **ignoring** all turnings until it widens and the going eases. Continue along the wide track to the road and follow this **SA** down the valley.

CONTINUES ON ON PAGE 117

p29 Lonscale Fell Loop

19 **Skiddaw Loop**
Part 1

FINISHES ON PAGE 115

Nether Row 307

Stott Ghyll

Wood Ho

Hudscales

Fell Side

Potts Gill

Wood Hall

Hutton Sceugh

373

Haltcliff Hall

Felside Brow

255

7 Mine (dis)

Mine (dis)

308

Deer Hills

Haltcliff Ho

6 Calebreck

Low Pike

West Fell

Haltcliff View

High Row

Caldbeck Fells

Birk Moss

High Pike 658

Mine (dis)

Carrock Beck

To 238

Bannest Hill

627

Linewath

n Crag

607° Miton Hill

Great Lingy Hill 616

Carrock Fell 661 fort

Stone Ends

Longdale

Round Knott

Coomb Height

Coomb

Mine

627

Cumbria Way

Swineside

5

Roundhouse

River Caldew

Mosed

Bowscale

4

CONTINUED FROM PAGE 115

32

Tarn Crags

Bowscale

Bowscal

19 Skiddaw Loop Part 2

5 Turn **L** at the T-junction in Mosedale and follow the road north. After 2.5km the road bends to the right, with a lone chevron sign warning drivers. Continue **SA** on to a track to cut the corner, and **SA** along the road as the track ends.

6 After a further 1.5km the road reaches a small lay-by just before a cattle grid. Turn **L** up the good track in the lay-by (**ignoring** the grassy bridleway going off left immediately after the start of the track). Follow this obvious track past two sets of old mine workings.

7 After the second old mine working, follow the track up a short, steep and straight climb and go **SA** over the vague crossroads just beyond. After 150m the track appears to end. Turn sharp **R** on to a vague grassy track to descend and climb over the small hill to the right. The track becomes more obvious as you crest the hill.

8 Descend fast, **ignoring** all turnings, to a T-junction with a loose stone track running alongside a wall. Turn **R** and descend through a gate to the road. Turn **L**.

9 After 2km, turn **L** over a small bridge with white railings on to a dead-end lane. Follow the lane and, as it swings right to a gate, continue **SA** on to a dirt track. Follow this to a gate just beyond a house and go through this to the road. Turn **L**.

10 Continue for 4km, passing two lanes on the right as you go. About 750m after the second turning, pass Peter House Farm in a small wood. Just beyond it, turn **L** on to a tarmac lane signed *Bridleway to Skiddaw House*.

11 Follow the lane for 1.5km until a wide stone track forks off **R**, signed *Bridleway to Skiddaw House and Threlkeld* on a large rock. Climb steeply up past Whitewater Dash to a gate.

12 Go through the gate and keep following the wide track, **ignoring** all turnings, until it descends and climbs to Skiddaw House. Bear **L** and then **R** to pass in front of the house and rejoin your outward route.

◄⊙⊃ **Making a day of it**

The **Lonscale Fell Loop** on page 29 makes a great alternative start to this ride, adding a little extra distance and a final fast descent into Keswick.

LONSCALE FELL

DROPPING BACK DOWN FROM BOREDALE HAUSE

20 High Street North

30km/19 miles

Introduction

A classic for mountain bikers! A trip up High Street is almost less about the riding and more about a big day out in the hills. After pushing or carrying your bike up a huge hill, the undulating ride along the northern half of High Street offers great views in every direction. It's a similar case on the return leg up Boredale – some carrying, but in a lovely setting and the rewards are some great views. It's not all about the views and 'getting out there' though. The descent from Loadpot Hill is seriously fast in places and features some flat-out singletrack, and the downhill run from the top of Boredale is as fast as you dare!

The Ride

You may as well leave the car park in the granny gear as you'll probably only find a couple of hundred metres of flat/down-hill riding in the first three kilometres! Grind your way up toward Hayeswater on a good track before swinging on to grass. The next grind up to The Knott is just that, but once you're up, you're up, and there are some great 360-degree views of virtually everywhere in the Lakes (almost!). Undulate along the ridge to the fast and swoopy descent off the end. Turn left towards Ullswater and speed down to Howtown and a choice of return routes: either climb up Boredale (with a push at the top) and speed down the other side, or pick your way along the technical bridleway skirting around the side of Ullswater. Easy tracks lead back to Hartsop.

ALTITUDE PROFILE

785

HIGH RAISE

BOREDDALE HAUSE

Metres

160

0 Km   5   10   15   20   25   30

HIGH STREET NORTH

GRADE: ▲

TOTAL DISTANCE: 30KM/19 MILES » **TOTAL ASCENT**: 1,220M/4,003FT » **START/FINISH**: HARTSOP
START GR: NY 410130 » **PARKING**: SMALL CAR PARK IN HARTSOP » **TIME**: 3-6 HOURS » **SATNAV**: CA11 0NZ
OS MAP: LANDRANGER 90 » **PUB**: NONE ON THE RIDE » **CAFE**: SANDWICH TIME.

20 **High Street North**

S→ From the parking area, go through the gate at the end (signed *Hayeswater*). The track starts as dirt (briefly) before becoming tarmac for a while. At the fork immediately after the cattle grid, bear **R** and descend to cross a bridge and start the first part of the climb proper.

2 The bridleway crosses the river and runs up the hillside for around 200m before reaching Hayeswater, but it's hard to spot. The easiest route is to continue to Hayeswater, turning **L** as you reach it to cross the footbridge – although this short section is a footpath, so act appropriately.

3 Keep going **SA** up the massive grassy hillside in front of you. The track is vague at first, but becomes more obvious higher up, crossing a broken wall and bearing to the **R**, becoming more rideable as it does so. (If in doubt, you are heading up on to the blunt ridge, and then to the left-hand side of, and behind, the knobby hill on your right.)

4 The track meets a wall and bears **L**. Follow it to a junction with a cairn and turn sharp **L** to climb up to Rampsgill Head. At the summit (jagged rocks), turn **L** and continue **SA**, descending and climbing on to High Raise. Drop down to a wall and follow it to the **R**. At the corner, cross the stile and continue. Go through a gate.

5 Follow the vague track, keeping the fence to your left and climb. Descend through a gap in the wall.

6 Climb and descend again and then, just before climbing on to Loadpot Hill (recognisable by the trig point on the summit), the bridleway bears **L**, passing the hill on its western side. If you miss the track and climb to the summit, you're on a footpath, but you can descend to meet the bridleway again by continuing **SA** over the hill.

7 Begin to descend. You'll reach a fork after about 1km – **ignore** the left-hand fork (which is the more obvious track and is probably covered in tyre tracks), and bear **R** on to a narrower, grassy track and continue to descend.

8 You will eventually reach a T-junction with an obvious track as the gradient eases (hill ahead). Turn **L** and follow this track as it weaves its way towards Ullswater. Follow the track as it becomes more defined for a fast descent.

9 Bear **L** where the track forks (the obvious track descends to the right) and ride to a gate by a house (signed *Cyclists, please walk*). Follow the track around to the **R** and turn **L** through a gate with a *bridleway* sign.

10 Cross the river and head up a short climb to a 4-way sign. Go **SA** signed *Public Bridleway Martindale House* along a grassy track that contours, descends and climbs. Keep going **SA** (**ignore** a left turn just before the second steep climb). Drop down to the church and the road. Turn **L** and then **R** at the junction, following signs for *Sandwick*.

11 Go **SA** at the hairpin, signed *Patterdale, Footpath Only*. At the end of the road, go **SA** through gates on to the obvious track. Steady climbing leads up a quiet valley with great views. You'll have to carry the last bit of the climb.

> **OR** Follow the hairpin round to the **R** and continue along the road. At the car park, turn **L** on to a bridleway signed *Bridlepath to Patterdale*. This soon turns to technical singletrack running around the edge of Ullswater. It eventually widens. Go **SA** through the gate at Side Farm and **SA** on to tarmac through the next gate. Follow the road round to the **R** and turn **L** at the main road. Ride to the houses at Bridgend and turn **L** on to a signed bridleway just before the last house. Follow this bridleway through gates, across fields and over the river to a good track. Turn **R** and return to Hartsop.

12 Follow the track round to the **R**, and then **SA** (south-west) across the plateau you have reached, heading for the lowest point at its 'open' (western) edge. **Ignore** turnings until you reach a small, smooth, flattish area. Continue **SA** across this (there's a bit of a gully on the left) and a wide, loose track will appear, descending very steeply towards Patterdale.

13 At the bottom, turn **L** (**SA**) along the wide track. At the road, turn **L** and climb back to Hartsop.

◀━▣━ Making a day of it
There are loads of options here. Ride the **Ullswater Singletrack** (page 35), continue south to ride the full **High Street** (page 151) or explore the bridleways at the northern end of the ride.

TIM RUSSON STARTING THE WALNA SCAR DESCENT TO CONISTON

21 Walna Scar

21km/13 miles

Introduction

This is a route for experienced mountain bikers, as it involves crossing high mountain country on very difficult technical ascents and descents. Expect to shoulder your bike, but believe me, it's all worth it in the end as you nail one of the classic Lakeland passes. This route only takes in half of the full Walna Scar Road. If you want to ride the entire thing (and it's well worth it) turn to page 67 and link this ride to the Broughton Moor & Seathwaite route, giving a great ride linking some fun trails from Coniston to Broughton Moor and then a return route up and over the full Walna Scar Road.

The Ride

We start in Coniston at the ferry terminal, mainly because the cafe there comes highly recommended – especially in winter when you're guaranteed a table! The route heads out towards the Coniston Hall Campsite then on to Torver. Once through Torver, some pleasant lanes climb steeply into woods and drop to the River Lickle via some sweet singletrack. An undulating climb on the west bank of the river leads to some seriously technical climbing – expect to shoulder your bike – up to meet the Walna Scar Road, which it follows up and over Walna Scar itself. It's then downhill all the way back to Coniston on this classic pass. For a completely different, but equally good challenge, try the route in reverse.

ALTITUDE PROFILE

610

Metres

50

0 Km   5   10   WALNA SCAR   15   20

WALNA SCAR

GRADE: ▲

TOTAL DISTANCE: 21KM/13 MILES » **TOTAL ASCENT**: 807M/2,648FT » **START/FINISH**: CONISTON FERRY TERMINAL
START GR: SD 308970 » **PARKING**: FERRY TERMINAL CAR PARK, LAKE ROAD, CONISTON » **TIME**: 2.5-4 HOURS
SATNAV: LA21 8AN » **OS MAP**: LANDRANGER 96 » **PUB**: VARIOUS IN CONISTON » **CAFE**: BLUEBIRD CAFE, CONISTON, TEL: 01539 441 649.

21 **Walna Scar**

⮊ From the car park, go back towards Coniston, over the bridge and, on the right-hand bend, go **L** through the double gate on to the cycleway to Torver.

2 Follow the cycleway to Coniston Hall Campsite. Continue through the campsite staying on the metalled road. Bear **L** at the fork towards the lake (a sign says *No camping beyond this point*). Pick up the cycleway again at the next gate, continuing through the field to a gate, following signs to *Torver*.

3 The track joins tarmac, which leads to a T-junction. Turn **R** and ride to the main road, passing over the old railway. Turn **L** towards Torver, ride through the village and turn **R** 1.5km after the village to climb steeply up a narrow lane.

4 At the forest, turn **R** through a gate at the forestry sign *Broughton Moor*. Descend to a right-hand bend and start to climb. **Ignore** the forest road on the left. On the brow of the climb turn **L** on to a semi-hidden bridleway to descend superb singletrack. At the junction with the forest road below, turn **L**. The forest road descends to cross a concrete bridge and then climbs steeply to another forest road. Turn **L** and then **R** **(easy to miss)** on to singletrack just after a right-hand bend. Follow this superb singletrack to drop steeply to another forest road.

5 Turn **R** then immediately **L** down a bridleway. Continue through the gate to the lane and turn **R**, crossing the bridge and climbing steeply to the farm (Stephenson Ground).

6 At the farm, turn **R** through a gate, signed *Bridleway*. After passing through the gate continue **SA** towards Walna Scar. (**Ignore** the bridleway on the left). The track becomes more arduous the further you go, but don't be put off – it's worth it! The bridleway follows a stream some metres below. After passing through the second gate just after a path junction the trail becomes more technical with a few dismounts likely unless you're a real talent! Eventually the bridleway crosses the stream to meet with the path/bridleway on the opposite side. Continue climbing **SA**. Bear **R** at the next path junction.

7 The ground becomes increasingly boggy, the worst of which can be avoided by taking the higher ground, especially in winter when keeping your feet dry is preferable! Skirt the bottom of a small crag before eventually reaching some ruined buildings (the area was once quarried for slate). Follow the obvious path between the buildings before heading out over the fell again.

8 There are a few choices of path but stay high, eventually meeting the well-maintained Walna Scar Road, now so big I'm sure it's visible from outer space! Turn **R** and climb steeply to the summit. It may be clear, it may not. How much did you ride? None of that matters now as the rest of the route is downhill into Coniston. How fast you go depends on you(!) but **be warned**, this road moves and changes according to how much rain there's been. Expect the unexpected – and walkers. The descent is steep, rocky and loose, has a huge drop-off and is worth every painful pedal and step you took to get to the top!

9 Eventually the 'road' reaches a car park and a gate. Continue **SA** on to a metalled lane which leads down into Coniston. At the very bottom continue **SA** over the main road and along Lake Road to return to the car park at the ferry terminal.

←☙☙ **Making a day of it**

Ride the full Walna Scar road (you know you want to!) by linking up with **Broughton Moor & Seathwaite** on page 67.

CONISTON WATER

Introduction

This is a route that should be on every mountain biker's tick list because of the dramatic location and amazing switchback descent. However, it's not one to be underestimated. It crosses remote, high Lakeland fells and requires a good level of fitness, self-sufficiency and technical ability. It's also probably best left to the summer months as the pass can hold snow even after it's gone from lower slopes. The climb up Gatescarth Pass may have you reaching for an ebike, or wishing you had one; however, once you start climbing Nan Bield Pass you will have to shoulder the bike for long periods so make sure you're able to do this easily with whatever your chosen bike is.

The Ride

The route starts in Staveley, as parking in the Kentmere Valley is very limited. We head north up the eastern side of the valley, out over Green Quarter before dropping down to Sadgill in Longsleddale. From here we start the crossing of Gatescarth Pass. Once 'summited' we can enjoy the welcome descent to Haweswater where we take the bridleway to Small Water and Nan Bield Pass. After pausing to admire the views and catch our breath we descend the switchbacks then onwards down seemingly endless playful singletrack in the upper Kentmere Valley.

Note: Be aware that you'll be pushing or carrying your bike for long periods on this route.

ALTITUDE PROFILE

710

Metres

GATESCARTH PASS

NAN BIELD PASS

100

0 Km — 5 — 10 — 15 — 20 — 25

NAN BIELD PASS GRADE ▲

TOTAL DISTANCE: 29KM/18 MILES » **TOTAL ASCENT**: 1,152M/3,780FT » **START/FINISH**: STAVELEY » **START GR**: SD 470987
PARKING: STAVELEY » **TIME**: 4–5 HOURS » **SATNAV**: LA8 9PD » **OS MAP**: LANDRANGER 90; LANDRANGER 97
PUB: EAGLE & CHILD, STAVELEY, TEL: 01539 821 320 » **CAFE**: WILF'S CAFE, STAVELEY, TEL: 01539 822 329.

⮕ From the weir in Staveley, cross the bridge to the east side of the river then turn immediately **L** along the singletrack lane. Stay on this lane all the way to the farm/ stables where it turns into a gravel track. Continue along this gravel track passing through three gates. At the third and final gate bear **R** up the bridleway and out on to the fell.

2 Stay on this bridleway and climb all the way to the gate at the top. From here it is relatively flat as we continue on to Green Quarter. After passing a ruin on the left we reach a path junction. Continue **SA** to the obvious gap in the wall. Follow this well-defined bridleway, through another gate, then climb up to the far corner of the stone walls visible in the distance. Reach a metal gate.

3 Follow the bridleway, which is still well defined but quite boggy in places even in dry weather. Pass through another gate then descend (quite steep in places) to arrive at another gate. Continue on following the fence/wall to eventually cross a stream and then a short sharp climb towards the main Kentmere/Sadgill track. Turn **R** through the gate on to the track.

4 Descend this wide stony track down to Sadgill, following the bridleway around to the **L** before bearing **R** and over the bridge, where I'm sure you'll be tempted to stop for a break! Once over the bridge, turn **L** on to Gatescarth Pass.

22 Nan Bield Pass

© CROWN COPYRIGHT AND/OR DATABASE RIGHT. ALL RIGHTS RESERVED. LICENCE NUMBER 100025218.

5 Navigation is now very straightforward all the way to Haweswater, as we'll be following Gatescarth Pass all the way. It starts gently but gradually gets steeper (with stone pitching near the top of the first section) to reach a gate after which we get a short respite. Stay on the main track (passing the bridleway from Mosedale on the right) before reaching a 'bike-friendly' gate. You'll need to put the bike on the rear wheel to get through.

6 Continue along the pass, climbing some quite steep switchbacks before finally topping out at another gate. Once on the other side you will reach a signpost. It is tempting to go left at this point but it is a footpath; the bridleway continues **SA**, but we are rewarded for doing so with an entertaining rocky descent with great views down to Haweswater. There is another bike-friendly gate around three-quarters of the way down, but we eventually reach the valley bottom. Turn **L** just before you reach the car park, signposted *Nan Bield Pass*.

7 This lower part of Nan Bield is mostly rideable and has a genuine feeling of remoteness. Remember to look back and take in the views of Haweswater Reservoir. A short steep section brings us to a gate; press on through the gate for the final push towards Small Water.

8 After following the stream up, the tarn finally comes in to view. Take a well-earned break as the climb is about to get a bit steeper from here! The bridleway goes anticlockwise around the tarn before starting to climb again to the col on the horizon.

9 The path becomes steep and rocky and a little vague in places so remember to keep looking up, so you know you're headed in the right direction. As long as you keep going forwards and upwards you will eventually reach the ridge and a small shelter – it can be windy and cold up here even in high summer!

10 If you've made it this far, well done! Stretching out in front of you is what it's all been about ... take a moment to enjoy the views all the way out to sea, the now infamous switchback descent, followed by singletrack stretching off seemingly endlessly into the far distance. Anyway, enough of that – let's ride this!

11 After the concentrated effort of the switchbacks, the trail gives way to flatter terrain with occasional techy sections. On the whole it's also firm and dry until the final steep little slope down to the gate and the valley bottom of Kentmere.

12 Cross the stream, use the narrow bridge if you prefer, and following the now firm wide track down the Kentmere Valley. We eventually reach a farm and tarmac for the first time in quite a while. Turn **L**. From here we can either continue along the bridle-way through the gate in front of us or remain on the road (bearing **R** at each junction). If you're feeling tired, the bridleway is actually the best option as it doesn't climb up but follows the valley bottom, joining the road further on.

13 As we approach Kentmere village, bear round to the **L** then **R** and down the hill to join the main valley road. Turn **L** and stay on the road to return to Staveley.

◄⊙⊙ Making a day of it
Head south-west to link up with **Ings & Winster** (page 61).

HEADING TOWARDS GATESCARTH PASS

Section 21

Killers

Character building …
We wouldn't go so far as to say that these loops could kill you, but they won't be much fun if you're not prepared. Allow plenty of time; stock up well on the calories and make sure you're firing on all four cylinders.

23 Parkamoor & Tilberthwaite   40km/25 miles

Introduction

A long(ish) ride circumnavigating Coniston Water. With the stunning views from Parkamoor, the remoteness of Blawith Fells, the exhilaration of descending Walna Scar Road, the shock of civilisation in Coniston, the man-made landscape of Tilberthwaite quarries and the sheer beauty of Tarn Hows, this ride never has a dull moment!

The Ride

Starting from the forestry car park at High Cross, the route takes us south through Grizedale on great forest trails and then out over Parkamoor. Dropping down into the hamlet of High Nibthwaite on a classic South Lakes descent, we continue south for a little while longer, before turning right to cross the River Crake. From here we climb away from Coniston Water on singletrack over Blawith Fells and Woodland Fell. Reaching the A593, the route passes through the hamlet of Torver (pub stop, if needed) and then leaves the road to start the climb up to Walna Scar. After a rocky descent into Coniston, we rejoin the A593 turning north heading for High Tilberthwaite. From here the route turns east to join the main Tarn Hows right of way which leads us back to Hawkshead Hill and finally High Cross.

ALTITUDE PROFILE

PARKAMOOR

WALNA SCAR ROAD

Metres

300

40

0 Km   5   10   15   20   25   30   35   40

PARKAMOOR & TILBERTHWAITE   GRADE: ▲

TOTAL DISTANCE: 40KM/25 MILES » **TOTAL ASCENT**: 1,284M/4,213FT » **START/FINISH**: HIGH CROSS, GRIZEDALE FOREST » **START GR**: SD 332986 » **PARKING**: HIGH CROSS CAR PARK » **TIME**: 4–7 HOURS **SATNAV**: LA22 0PW » **OS MAP**: LANDRANGER 90; LANDRANGER 96 » **PUB**: SEVERAL ALONG THE ROUTE **CAFE**: SEVERAL IN CONISTON.

23 Parkamoor & Tilberthwaite

Directions – Parkamoor & Tilberthwaite

➲ Leave High Cross car park on the forest road at the far end of the car park (away from the road), heading south into Grizedale. Continue **SA** on a narrower trail as the track bends left after a short climb. Follow this trail until it rejoins a forest road.

2 Turn **R** and continue **SA** for 1.5km across Monk Coniston Moor, passing a track on the right and climbing to a T-junction. Turn **R**, uphill, passing a second bridleway on the right as you descend to an offset crossroads. Turn **R** and then fork **R** almost immediately.

3 Continue along the forest track, passing a bridleway on the right, to a sharp left-hand bend. Continue **SA** between three large boulders on to singletrack, marked with a bridleway sign to *Parkamoor*.

4 Follow this singletrack to the edge of the forest. Go through a gate on to an obvious trail out over Parkamoor, soon descending to a ruin. Pass in front of the ruin and descend between walls to a gate by a stream. Go through the gate in a ghostly type way and climb the hill ahead to a track. Turn **R** downhill (south) to start the superb South Lakes descent to High Nibthwaite.

5 Reaching High Nibthwaite in one piece, join the minor road and turn **L**. After 850m turn **R** on to a minor road opposite Arklid Farm. Cross the River Crake to join the A5084. Turn **L** on to the main road and continue south for another 850m to the village of Blawith.

6 Turn **R** up the minor lane opposite the church/phonebox/letterbox. Bear **R** at the fork and continue uphill. At the next fork after a cattle grid, bear **R** again. (The left branch is signed *Tottlebank only*.) After 800m the road reaches a T-junction. Turn **R** then immediately **L** on to a narrow bridleway signed *Woodland*.

7 Follow the obvious track, ignoring turnings, for some superb riding and climb to the highest point on Woodland Fell. At the summit, **ignore** a path to the left and keep to the bridleway. The descent doesn't fail to impress either but take care in your enthusiasm not to miss the **R** turn, marked by a small tree, after 900m.

8 The bridleway descends to cross a small river, and then climbs slightly to avoid a rather strangely positioned fence. Continue along this track, following the wall to a sharp left turn where the path climbs steeply, staying by the wall. At the top bear **R**, dropping to a small stream with a steep entry and exit (be sure to select the right gear). After fording the stream, the path bears **L** through a gap in the fence. Drop down before climbing to meet the main track. Turn **R** and climb along this before descending to Haveriggholme.

9 At the foot of the descent, pass through two gates and join a metalled road. Follow this road for 2.8km to the A593. At the main road, turn **R** to Torver.

10 Follow the A593 through Torver (pub stop, if required) to a right-hand bend just outside the village. Turn **L** up a lane and climb the hill. Follow the lane, keeping **L** at the forks, climbing up around the right-hand hairpin and on to a signposted bridle-way. The lane soon becomes a track with some quite challenging rocky steps and steep sections, but all good fun! Eventually the bridleway passes through a sheep-fold and crosses a stream via a bridge. The bridleway then starts to climb through an old slate quarry.

11 At the top of this lung-busting ascent (more due to loose slate than to its length or steepness) the path becomes more forgiving. A fence appears on the left, preventing you from falling head first into a now-flooded disused quarry. Round this fence and continue the ascent. After a rather difficult rock step there is a choice of route. It's not crucial which path you choose, as they all lead to the main Walna Scar Road, but the preferred way is to bear **R**, drop down to the stream and climb the steep grassy bank in front of you and off to the right.

12 Upon reaching Walna Scar Road (the big wide track), regardless of your choice of route, turn **R**, descend to join tarmac and continue down into Coniston and a well-earned cafe stop (if you stopped in Torver as well then you're just being greedy). Drop into Coniston until you hit the main A593 Ambleside road. Turn **L** towards Ambleside.

13 Following the A593 go over the bridge in Coniston and turn **L** by the Black Bull pub. Where the road becomes unmade, turn **R** on to a bridleway. Follow this until it finishes on the A593, and turn **L** immediately on to a road signposted *Tilberthwaite*. Follow this road to its end at High Tilberthwaite Farm. **Please dismount** and walk through the farmyard, taking the gate on the **R** once in the yard itself.

14 Follow the well-made track, keeping **R** at the fork, for 1km and descend sharply to a T-junction. Turn **R** and descend, cross a stream and tackle the tricky climb. Turn **R** on to the main track at the top and climb to a metalled lane at some buildings.

15 Turn **L**, climbing around an S-bend and turn **R** right up the track to a gate. Continue **SA** along the track to its end at High Oxen Fell (farm). Go through the farm on to the metalled lane, bearing **R** at the junction and dropping down to the A593.

16 Cross the road with care and climb **SA** up the lane opposite, taking the **R** fork after a few metres on to a rough track. This is the main Tarn Hows/Arnside Intake right of way, so expect to meet motorised vehicles! Follow it for over 3km (tricky climbing and a fast descent) to its end at Knipe Fold. At the T-junction with the road, turn **R**. Climb up Hawkshead Hill, **ignoring** turnings to the left and right and, after 1.5km, continue **SA** over the main road into the car park at High Cross.

◄◉◉◉ Making a day of it
You could tack the **Blawith Loop** (page 5) on to the southern end of this ride, explore **Walna Scar** (page 127) to the west or play in the forest on the eastern side of the route.

Introduction

High Street is one of the most spectacular and enjoyable rides in the Lake District. There are many ways of tackling it and this is probably one of the most arduous. The route follows the stunning ridge, taking the course of the old Roman road over High Street, High Raise and Wether Hill, then off towards Bampton Grange. The isolation of Swindale and Mosedale is breathtaking and is an area of the Lakes not often visited. It would be unusual to meet anyone here. This is a tough ride over high mountain terrain. Although not technically demanding, riders undertaking this route should be used to a long day. For the sake of route finding and enjoying the fantastic views, pick a clear day. You will need map-reading skills.

The Ride

This ride starts in Ings as it has a fine pub with a choice of ales (for when you get back). Getting to High Street always involves a climb and this route takes you up Park Fell with (more than) a bit of a push before following the old Roman road to Wether Hill. Vague trails lead to The Pen, and farm lanes to Bampton Grange. Country lanes take you down the beautiful Swindale Valley until the valley rears up and you find yourself pushing again. Vague trails lead to Mosedale Cottage (owned by the Mountain Bothies Association, and where you can spend the night if you wish). The trail becomes vague until you reach a gate, when it becomes non-existent. Join the Gatescarth Pass, head to Sadgill and continue to Kentmere and a choice of finishes – Garburn Pass being one of them!

ALTITUDE PROFILE

HIGH STREET   **GRADE:** ▲▲

TOTAL DISTANCE: 60KM/37 MILES » **TOTAL ASCENT**: 1,932M/6,339 FT » **START/FINISH**: WATERMILL INN, INGS
START GR: SD 444987 » **PARKING**: ROADSIDE PARKING IN INGS (PARKING MAY BE LIMITED, PARTICULARLY AT WEEKENDS); PLEASE PARK RESPONSIBLY » **TIME**: ALL DAY! » **SATNAV**: LA8 9PY » **OS MAP**: LANDRANGER 90; LANDRANGER 97
PUB: WATERMILL INN, INGS, TEL: 01539 821 309 » **CAFE**: WILF'S CAFE, STAVELEY, TEL: 01539 822 329.

Directions – High Street

⮕ From Ings, cross the road via the cycle path. Turn **R** at Hill Farm, signed *High Borrans, Moor Howe Lane.*

2 Continue along this road for 3km. Look out for a sign to *High Borrans* on the right. Shortly after this sign as the road bears to the left, turn **R** on to a wide bridleway to Dubbs Reservoir. Follow this good bridleway for 2.5km, passing Dubbs Reservoir, and turn **L** back on yourself (straight ahead through the gate is the Garburn Pass) for a fun downhill.

3 After 500m turn sharp **R** and head north along the valley until the river can be crossed, via a footbridge by an old building, to another track. Turn **R** and head north on this, don't look too far ahead: you may not want to see where you're going!

4 As you approach Park Fell, the gradient starts to rear up quite considerably and by the time you go through a gate in a wall (continue **SA**) you will probably be pushing your bike (there is about half an hour of very steep terrain). As the wall curves away to the left, bear **R** on the bridleway, climbing steeply.

5 The bridleway eventually relents. Keep going north-north-east to join the main track from Froswick. Turn **L**. At the two metal fence posts, bear **R** on the bridleway as the ground falls steeply away to the right (**ignore** the well-trodden footpath that bears towards Thornthwaite Beacon). Continue **SA** until, after a short distance, the bridleway splits again. Take the **L** fork.

6 The main bridleway takes you to below the summit of High Street on good, obvious tracks, and then heads north downhill to a junction of two bridleways. Turn **R** (north-east). You get a stunning view of Hayeswater at this point. Follow good tracks along the ridge, leading north to High Raise, Red Crag and Wether Hill.

CONTINUES ON PAGE 156

CONTINUED FROM PAGE 153

154 LAKE DISTRICT MTB – ESSENTIAL TRAILS

CONTINUED FROM PAGE 157

FINISHES ON PAGE 153

24 **High Street Part 2**

CONTINUED FROM PAGE 154

CONTINUES ON PAGE 155

24 **High Street**
Part 3

7 As you descend from Wether Hill you will probably be on a track to the left of the main bridleway. You need to fork **R** at **GR NY 458174** on a bridleway before beginning to climb. The bridleway is, unfortunately, not easily visible on the ground. If you start going uphill and arrive at a cairn that is part of the old ruin you have gone too far. Follow the bridleway to contour around the hill without losing too much height. Eventually you will be able to see two vague trails ahead on The Pen. Take the **L** trail for a great down-hill. You should pass a cairn to your right in the middle of a field, do not go to this, it seems to be there for no reason. (If it is on your left you are on the wrong track.)

8 At the good farm track by Keldhead, turn **R** and **R** again at the road. Go over a cattle grid and through a gate at Rough Hill Farm. Bear **R** through the buildings to another gate and continue on a gated road to a T-junction. Turn **L** and follow the road to Bampton (village store and cafe). Turn **R** at the T-junction and keep **L** at the next to Bampton Grange (pub). Just before the sharp left turn over the bridge, turn **R**, bearing **L** at the next junction, signed *Swindale*.

9 Continue along this lane for just over 1km and turn **R**, signed *Swindale 3 miles*. This lane takes you to the idyllic spot of Swindale. Continue **SA** at a crossroads on to a gated road for 4km to Swindale Head. As the road ends, continue riding **SA** for a short distance until it is no longer possible; a short(ish) push then brings you to the top of Nabs Crag. The trail now becomes vague, so contour round to the **L** of the craggy knoll and then bear back **R** to a fence with a gate at the right-hand side.

10 Once through the gate, the bridleway is a little better defined and follows the line of an old wall. **Ignore** the obvious trail, which takes you to a footbridge (although if you do find yourself here, do not cross the bridge but bear back **R**, to rejoin the main trail). From here the trail leads to Mosedale Cottage. This bothy is always open but **please clear up after yourself** if you use the facility (for further information: *www.mountainbothies.org.uk*).

11 The trail from here is tough going due to the nature of the terrain and can be boggy after wet weather. Head towards a gated fence on vague trails. Beyond the gate, the trail becomes non-existent. Take a compass bearing of **252°** and head downhill – carefully, as you will have to change course and wind your way through this boggy and craggy terrain.

12 Finally you reach the more obvious Gatescarth Pass at the bottom of the valley. Did you find the bridleway sign? Were you above it, below it or on it? Turn **L** and head downhill fast. This terrain is hard on your arms, not technical, but a long descent, with lots of vibration.

13 At Sadgill, turn **R** over the bridge, turning **L** shortly afterwards at the *bridleway* sign and then **R** in front of the farm to a gate. The track climbs gradually in a southerly direction through Sadgill Wood and then on to another gate.

14 Beyond the gate, continue **SA** up the steep track. (**Ignore** the bridleway to the left.) This is a good technical downhill, but unfortunately you're going up it! The track eventually plateaus and a fun downhill ensues (with a few gates). You eventually join the road at High Lane. Turn **L** through a gate on to a fast downhill – **be careful** here as the bends are blind to cars. Follow the road down and turn **L** (south) on to the Kentmere-Staveley road in the direction of Staveley. After approx. 4.5km, and after crossing the bridge over the river, turn **L** towards Staveley. Keep **R** at junctions in Staveley and turn **R** again on to the cycleway adjacent to the A591 to return to Ings. Phew!

> **OR** **Option 1**. Turn **R** at the first road (goes back acutely) and descend to Low Bridge. Turn **R** to Kentmere Church. If you're not tired enough at this point, continue over the Garburn Pass (see pages 20–22 for directions) and back to your car.

> **OR** **Option 2**. However, if you are a little fatigued, take the bridleway to the **L** of the church and descend to Kentmere Hall. Go through the gate and struggle uphill – on good trails so no getting off apart from at the gates! After Whiteside End, an undulating, mainly downhill trail leads to a gate in a wall. Bear **R** over the stream as the bridleway forks and follow the good trail over open fell and through gates until a gate with signposts. Turn **L**, signed *Grassgarth* for another exhilarating downhill. At the fork, bear **R**, eventually leading to Grassgarth and a metalled road. Follow this back to Ings.

Section 5

Bonus Section

» The North Face Trail, Grizedale Forest
» Whinlatter Forest, Keswick
» Top Tens

WHINLATTER FOREST, ABOVE KESWICK

The North Face Trail, Grizedale Forest

The 16-kilometre red-graded The North Face trail was officially opened in 2006 and was the first purpose-built trail in the Lake District National Park. It originally featured a lot more boardwalk sections; these divided riders' opinions at the time, as some found them problematic while others just enjoyed the test. The Forestry Commission has since removed a number of these sections to give us the trail we have today.

The Route

The trailhead is at the now redeveloped visitor centre in the heart of the forest. Signage is clear and very easy to follow, consisting of a white arrow on a red background – red for The North Face.

Climbing out away from the visitor centre, the trail crosses a cattle grid, turns right and then takes an acute left into the forest. This is the start of nine sections of singletrack, each with a name, such as *Topsy Turvy* and *Up on the Boardwalk*. The route is technical in places but these sections are worked into the trail and not artificial sections running alongside.

While only 10 miles long, the trail can be linked with the abundance of bridleways and byways that criss-cross Grizedale Forest, to give some of the best riding the South Lakes has to offer. Just go explore and mix it up a bit!

Getting there

From Ambleside, head west on the A593 towards Coniston, and soon turn left in Clappersgate on to the B5286 towards Hawkshead. Head south through Hawkshead and turn right up a tiny lane, signposted to *Grizedale*, just as you leave the houses. The visitor centre is on your right after approximately 3 kilometres.

Grid Ref: **SD 335943**
Sat Nav: **LA22 0QJ**
Facilities: **Car parking (pay and display), cafe, toilets, bike hire, bike shop, visitor centre.**

For more information go to:
www.forestryengland.uk/grizedale/the-north-face-mtb-trail-grizedale
Grizedale Visitor Centre: **03000 674 495**

Grizedale Mountain Bikes (on site):
01229 860 335
www.grizedalemountainbikes.co.uk

Whinlatter Forest, Keswick

The 19-kilometre red-graded Altura-sponsored trail in Whinlatter Forest officially opened in 2008 and claims to 'put the mountain back into mountain biking'. Expect a Scottish-style trail here, very different to Grizedale. Bursting with its own character it will have you returning over and over again! The 7.5-kilometre blue-graded Quercus trail was added in 2009 and is less technical than the Altura but still a real mountain bikers' trail, full of surprises. Combining both makes for a great day of riding.

Altura Trail

The trailhead is at the visitor centre, with the start at the far end beyond the cycle shop. Signage is clear and consists of a red arrow on a white background. In order to enjoy this trail to the max a reasonable level of fitness and bike handling skills are required. The route is divided into two main sections, north and south. The north is the original and, like England itself, very different in character to the south! The north side is tight and twisty and technically challenging, while the south side is a bit more open; a wider trail, more swoopy and flowing, certainly on the descent. Along the route you'll find additional obstacles to challenge your skills further. Why not stop and play for a while? Don't forget to take in some of the best views of any trail centre in the UK …

Quercus Trail

Starting from the same location as the Altura trail, follow the blue arrows on a white background. This trail is tamer than the Altura and starts with a descent for a refreshing change! The singletrack is fun to ride and suitable for more adventurous families with confident little riders. Along the route you will also find short technical sections to have a bit of fun on. After crossing the road you'll reach a signed shortcut, especially useful if you have children with you, as beyond this junction the trail does become a tad more challenging.

Getting there

From Keswick, take the A66 west towards Cockermouth. After a couple of kilometres, enter Braithwaite and immediately turn left on the B5292. Follow the road through the village and up into Whinlatter Forest. The car park and visitor centre are eventually on your right.

Grid Ref:	**NY 209245**
Sat Nav:	**CA12 5TW**
Facilities:	**Car parking (pay and display), toilets, bike hire, bike shop, bike wash, visitor centre, cafe.**

For more information go to:
www.forestryengland.uk/whinlatter
Cyclewise (on site): **01768 778 711**
www.cyclewise.co.uk

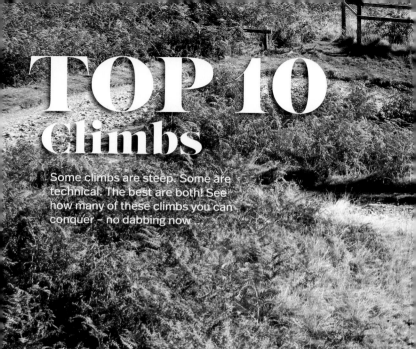

TOP 10
Climbs

Some climbs are steep. Some are technical. The best are both! See how many of these climbs you can conquer – no dabbing now …

1

Moor Howe to Garburn Pass Summit
Some quite technical sections as you start to tire.

Route 4: NY 423006–NY 435044

2

Kiln Bank Cross to Raven's Crag
Looks impossible but in fact gives in quite easily to strong legs!

Route 12: SD 214932–SD 224922

3

Miterdale Head to Tongue Moor
Bit of a push to get going, then it's just a matter of how high you want your heart rate to go.

Route 14: NY 159025–NY 173036

4

Sadgill to Cocklaw Fell
Take a break at the river before you grind your way up this one. After the gate where the bridleway divides is a special challenge – some steep, technical ground; gold star if you get up!

Route 8: NY 483057–NY 479049

5

A593/Arnside to Iron Keld
From the A593 this steep bridleway grinds away through reasonably technical terrain.

Route 13: NY 335029–NY 337011

6
7
8
9
0

High Tilberthwaite
Route 13: NY 307014–NY 308023
Short, steep and rocky. Might take more than one attempt, but is completely doable.

Low Bank Ground to Lawson Park
Route 18: SD 317968–SD 322950
The reverse of the downhill, this time the gates give a welcome rest.

Black Combe
Route 5: SD 131827–SD 134855
A real leg burner; the start is very steep, so maybe try to save your legs. Not technical – it's all good tracks – it's just very steep.

Skiddaw House
Route 19: NY 249323–NY 272313
Climb the broad track from Peter House Farm. Technically easy, but with a steep bit just before the gate.

Robin Lane to Hundreds Road
Route 10: NY 407026–NY 397023
A good beginners' climb on which to see if the legs are up to more arduous work.

1   Garburn Pass to Kentmere   Route 4: NY 435044–NY 454044
Monster descent with some good man-laid obstacles; steep with great hairpins.

2   Parkamoor to High Nibthwaite   Route 23: SD 306924–SD 294898
Long descent on a good track; not too technical but fast.

3   'The Fox' to Esthwaite   Route 18: SD 345952–SD 357955
Starts off with undulating terrain, then really kicks off with some varying technical sections.

4   Skiddaw Summit to car park   Route 6b: NY 261291–NY 281254
A high-speed descent from the summit of one of Lakeland's best known peaks! Beware of dogs, sheep, children and walkers en route …

5   Lawson Park to Low Bank Ground   Route 18: SD 322950–SD 317968
If it weren't for the gate this would be one of the best downhills anywhere – nothing technical, just fast.

TOP 10
Downhills

This list is by no means exhaustive and we're sure that other riders will have their own ideas. These are our pick of the best and they're all legal, all rideable and all easy to find.

6

Walna Scar to Coniston   Route 21: SD 258964–SD 301974

Stupendous, some good steep hairpins and technical rock steps; lower your saddle and enjoy.

7

Whiteside End to Kentmere Hall Farm   Route 4: NY 447029–NY 451042

Just let the brakes off and go. Mind the right-hander at the end!

8

Natty Bridge to Stephenson Ground   Route 21: SD 242946–SD 235932

Starts just above Natty Bridge where the footpath and bridleway split. Exposed start; superb singletrack downhill thereafter.

9

Nan Bield Pass   Route 22: NY 452096–NY 456070

Infamous switchback descent, followed by singletrack, from the summit of Nan Bield Pass down to the valley near Kentmere.

0

Watendlath to Rosthwaite   Route 17: NY 270160–NY 259150

Steep and rocky. Make that *very* steep and *very* rocky!

TOP 10
Singletrack

Lakeland singletrack varies from the wooded to the moorland and then to the man-made. Some are swoopy, some are tricky – they're all fun. Check out these suggestions for our pick of the best.

1. Hazelseat to Low Dale Park
Route 18: SD 368924–SD 350918

2.5 kilometres of woodland singletrack, starting with a wide and steep climb before narrowing at the summit. Fantastic steep singletrack descent out of the forest on to open land.

2. Martindale
Route 7: NY 416156–NY 434165

Perfect white singletrack over the top of the ridge leads to a fast grassy descent into Martindale.

3. Broughton Moor
Route 12: SD 246928–SD 238929

Short and sweet with a fast descent, this will have you wishing for more!

4. Appletree Holme to Climb Stile
Route 1: SD 277888–SD 258897

3.6 kilometres of superb Lakeland singletrack across open fell. It doesn't get much better than this!

5. Kiln Bank Cross to Stephenson Ground
Route 12: SD 214933–SD 235932

Classic Lakeland singletrack across open fell. A distance of 3.8 kilometres.

6
Witherslack Hall to Witherslack　　　Route 9: SD 435859–SD 435835

Ok, so it's not all singletrack, but once you're in the trees you won't care a bit! Very fast in summer; watch out for horses and limestone when it's wet. Distance is 2 kilometres.

7
Altura Trail and Quercus Trail, Whinlatter Forest

A great mix of man-made trails, with many obstacles along the way to test your skills further.

8
Lonscale Fell　　　Route 6a: NY 292280–NY 293261

Fast narrow bits, technical climbs, slippery rock (in the wet) and a massive drop to one side.

9
Mosedale　　　Route 19: NY 287291–NY 313314

Fast, rutted, rocky, grassy, sketchy ... and it goes on for ages.

0
The North Face Trail, Grizedale Forest

The first purpose-built trail in Cumbria. A mix of singletrack, forest road and wooden obstacles. No walkers to worry about either!

Appendix

TOURIST INFORMATION CENTRES

www.lakedistrict.gov.uk
www.visitlakedistrict.com

Ambleside . . . . T: **01539 468 135**
Bowness . . . . T: **08459 010 845**
Carlisle . . . . T: **01228 598 596**
Cockermouth . . . . T: **01900 822 634**
Coniston . . . . T: **01539 441 533**
Hawkshead . . . . T: **01539 436 946**
Kendal . . . . T: **01539 735 891**
Keswick . . . . T: **08459 010 845**
Penrith . . . . T: **01768 867 466**
Ullswater . . . . T: **08459 010 845**

WEATHER

www.metoffice.gov.uk
www.mwis.org.uk

BIKE SHOPS

Biketreks, Grizedale and Ings T: **01539 431 245**
Wheelbase, Staveley . . . . . . T: **01539 821 443**
Velo Ulverston, Ulverston . . . T: **01229 581 116**
Ghyllside Cycles, Ambleside T: **01539 433 592**
Grizedale Mountain Bikes, . . T: **01229 860 335**
Grizedale

Cyclewise, Whinlatter . . . . . . T: **01768 778 711**
Keswick Bikes, ... T: **01768 773 355**
Keswick

4Play Cycles, Cockermouth T: **01900 823 377**

BIKE HIRE

Forgotten your bike?

Wheelbase, Staveley . . . . . . T: **01539 821 443**
Grizedale Mountain Bikes, . . T: **01229 860 335**
Grizedale

Cyclewise, Whinlatter . . . . . . T: **01768 778 711**
Keswick Bikes, ... T: **01768 773 355**
Keswick

Windermere Canoe Kayak, T: **01539 444 451**
Windermere

Country Lanes, Windermere T: **01539 444 544**

FOOD AND DRINK
Cafes

There are hundreds of cafes around, so we have only listed two of our favourites. As you are probably aware the majority of pubs also have good catering, particularly in the Lake District. See individual rides for more.

Wilf's Cafe, Staveley . . . . . . T: **01539 822 329**
Bluebird Cafe, Coniston . . . T: **01539 441 649**

Pubs

Again, there are loads – there's pretty much one in every village. See the individual rides for our recommendations. Here is a list of a few:

Eagle & Child, Staveley . . . . . T: **01539 821 320**
Watermill Inn, Ings . . . . T: **01539 821 309**
Golden Rule, Ambleside . . . . T: **01539 432 257**
Woolpack Inn, Eskdale . . . . . T: **01946 723 230**
Gilpin Bridge Inn, ... T: **01539 552 206**
Gilpin Bridge

Masons Arms, Cartmel Fell . . T: **01539 568 486**
Red Lion, Lowick Bridge . . . . T: **01229 885 366**
The Eagles Head, ... T: **01229 860 237**
Satterthwaite

Newfield Inn, Seathwaite . . . T: **01229 716 208**

ACCOMMODATION
Hostels
www.yha.org.uk
www.independenthostels.co.uk

YHA Ambleside .... T: **03453 719 620**
YHA Borrowdale .... T: **03453 719 624**
YHA Buttermere .... T: **03453 719 508**
YHA Coniston Holly How .... T: **03453 719 511**
YHA Coniston Coppermines T: **03453 719 630**
Derwentwater .... T: **01768 777 246**
Independent Hostel

Elterwater Hostel .... T: **01539 437 245**
YHA Ennerdale .... T: **03453 719 116**
YHA Eskdale .... T: **03453 719 317**
YHA Grasmere .... T: **03453 719 319**
Butharlyp Howe

YHA Hawkshead .... T: **03453 719 321**
YHA Helvellyn .... T: **03453 719 742**
YHA Honister Hause .... T: **03453 719 522**
Kendal Hostel .... T: **01539 724 066**
YHA Keswick .... T: **03453 719 746**
YHA Langdale .... T: **03453 719 748**
YHA Patterdale .... T: **03453 719 337**
Skiddaw House .... T: **07747 174 293**
YHA Wasdale Hall .... T: **03453 719 350**
YHA Windermere .... T: **03453 719 352**

Hotels, Self-Catering and B&B

Your best bet is to contact the Tourist Information Centre nearest to where you plan to ride, or search the internet.

Camping

There are campsites all over the Lake District. All you've got to do is get a map, look for camping symbols and find one you like. They vary tremendously depending on what you're looking for and are very easy to find, so we're not going to list any here.

WINDERMERE FERRY
(For Claife and Grizedale)

Summer Weekday 06:50, every 20mins, until 21:50
Summer Sunday 08:50, every 20mins, until 21:50
Winter Weekday 06:50, every 20mins, until 20:50
Winter Sunday 08:50, every 20mins, until 20:50

OTHER PUBLICATIONS

Great Britain Mountain Biking
Tom Fenton & Andy McCandlish,
Vertebrate Publishing
www.v-publishing.co.uk

Yorkshire Dales Mountain Biking
Nick Cotton, Vertebrate Publishing
www.v-publishing.co.uk

Peak District Mountain Biking
Jon Barton, Vertebrate Publishing
www.v-publishing.co.uk

Traffic-Free Cycle Trails
Nick Cotton, Vertebrate Publishing
www.v-publishing.co.uk

Pennine Bridleway
Hannah Collingridge, Vertebrate Publishing
www.v-publishing.co.uk

Swimming Wild in the Lake District
Suzanna Cruickshank, Vertebrate Publishing
www.v-publishing.co.uk

More than just a café ...

Serving excellent pre or post-ride breakfasts, lunches, homemade cakes and afternoon teas.

Open 7 days a week 9am – 4pm

Also available for takeaways when open and pre-ordered 'Wilf's Away' meals.

Wilf's Café

Staveley Mill Yard
Staveley
Cumbria
LA8 9LR

T 01539 822329

E food@wilfs-cafe.co.uk

www.wilfs-cafe.co.uk

ABOUT THE AUTHORS

Richard Staton started mountain biking back in Bristol in 1991 on a Trek 970 while on a student work placement from Sheffield City Polytechnic. Being based most of the time in Sheffield, those early years were spent riding in the Peak District. After graduation he moved to the South Lakes where he stayed in order to feed his addiction. Years later, he's still here and still ridin'!

Chris Gore is better known for his rock climbing escapades. It is little known that he has been riding bikes since his first tricycle, starting in London and finally seeing good sense and finishing in the Lakes (there are no mountains in London). Chris enjoys both road and MTB and throws himself down rocky slopes on a regular basis. Hey, it's faster than walking!

VERTEBRATE PUBLISHING

At Vertebrate Publishing we publish books to inspire adventure.

It's our rule that the only books we publish are those that we'd want to read or use ourselves. We endeavour to bring you beautiful books that stand the test of time and that you'll be proud to have on your bookshelf for years to come.

The Peak District was the inspiration behind our first books. Our offices are situated on its doorstep, minutes away from world-class climbing, biking and hillwalking. We're driven by our own passion for the outdoors, for exploration, and for the natural world; it's this passion that we want to share with our readers.

We aim to inspire everyone to get out there. We want to connect readers – young and old – with the outdoors and the positive impact it can have on well-being. We think it's particularly important that young people get outside and explore the natural world, something we support through our publishing programme.

As well as publishing award-winning new books, we're working to make available many out-of-print classics in both print and digital formats. These are stories that we believe are unique and significant; we want to make sure that they continue to be shared and enjoyed. *www.v-publishing.co.uk*